TWELVE
MODERN DRAMATISTS

by

RAYMOND COWELL, B.A., Ph.D.

*Senior Lecturer in English, Trinity
and All Saints' Colleges, Leeds*

PERGAMON PRESS

OXFORD · LONDON · EDINBURGH · NEW YORK
TORONTO · SYDNEY · PARIS · BRAUNSCHWEIG

Pergamon Press Ltd., Headington Hill Hall, Oxford
4 & 5 Fitzroy Square, London W.1

Pergamon Press (Scotland) Ltd., 2 & 3 Teviot Place, Edinburgh 1

Pergamon Press Inc., 44–01 21st Street, Long Island City, New York 11101

Pergamon of Canada, Ltd., 6 Adelaide Street East, Toronto, Ontario

Pergamon Press (Aust.) Pty. Ltd., 20–22 Margaret Street, Sydney,
New South Wales

Pergamon Press S.A.R.L., 24 rue des Écoles, Paris 5e

Vieweg & Sohn GmbH, Burgplatz 1, Braunschweig

Printed in Great Britain by A. Wheaton & Co. Ltd, Exeter and London

CONTENTS

ACKNOWLEDGEMENTS

EXTRACT from *Ghosts* is reprinted with the permission of Charles Scribner's Sons and William Heinemann Ltd. from the Archer translation of *The Collected Works of Henrik Ibsen*.

Extract from *Miss Julie* is reprinted by permission of Collins-Knowlton-Wing and Constable & Co. © 1966 by Elizabeth Sprigge. No public performance may take place without prior consent of A. P. Watt and Son.

Extract from *Uncle Vanya* reprinted by permission of Gerald Duckworth and Co.

Extract from *Saint Joan* reprinted by permission of The Society of Authors.

Extract from *Juno and the Paycock* from Sean O'Casey, *Collected Plays*, with permission of Macmillan & Co. Ltd.

Extract from *The Good Woman of Setzuan* © Copyright 1947, 1948, 1956, 1961 by Eric Bentley; Epilogue © Copyright 1965 by Eric Bentley. Originally published in the volume *Parables for the Theatre: Two Plays by Bertolt Brecht* by the University of Minnesota Press. Reprinted by permission.

Extract from *The Death of a Salesman* Copyright 1949 by Arthur Miller. Reprinted by permission of the Viking Press, Inc. and Elaine Greene Ltd.

Extract from *Roots* © Copyright 1959 by Arnold Wesker. Reprinted from *The Wesker Trilogy* by permission of Random House, Inc. and Jonathan Cape Ltd.

Extract from *Waiting for Godot* reprinted by permission of Faber and Faber Ltd. and Les Editions de Minuit.

Extract from *Rhinoceros* reprinted by permission of Grove

Press, Inc. and Calder and Boyars Ltd. Copyright © 1960 by John Calder (Publishers) Ltd.

Extract from *The Caretaker* reprinted by permission of Grove Press Inc. and Methuen & Co. Ltd. from *The Caretaker and The Dumb Waiter: Two Plays by Harold Pinter*. Copyright © 1960 by Theatre Promotions Ltd.

PREFACE

MUCH is heard nowadays of the need to broaden Sixth Form studies and Further Education, and courses on the Science side bear the brunt of such criticism. The danger of narrow specialization is just as real on the Arts side, however, and in English, for example, the 'set book' approach to A-level, if not supplemented by further and wider reading, can be quite disenchanting to the Sixth Former who is eager to come to grips with literature and the techniques of literary criticism. The purpose of this collection of extracts from the drama of the last eighty years or so is to provide in a convenient form a wide range of material which can be used concurrently with set books throughout a Sixth Form course in English or similar courses. The book has its origin in Sixth Form English teaching and in efforts to provide stimulating material for the growing literary interests of the Sixth Form pupil. It has been found that the wider reading involved enriches and deepens the individual's approach to the set books.

I hope, too, that the book may prove useful in General Studies courses in the Sixth Form: I have found it so. The material and the approach have also been found useful in Adult Education work and this further suggests that this collection might perhaps make some contribution to the work of Colleges of Education and to, for example, Liberal Studies courses in Technical Colleges.

The aim throughout has been to provide episodes which make an immediate impact, which are sufficiently long to involve the reader emotionally and which are of sufficient subtlety to repay close study. It is hoped, too, that the method of arrangement will illustrate the main streams of modern dramatic development. The questions and discussion points are intended to be simply starting points, for all the episodes deal with topics which are still current today, and they have been found to spark off wide-ranging discussions.

R.C.

INTRODUCTION:
THE DEVELOPMENT OF
MODERN DRAMA

It is always hazardous to speculate about future opinions of contemporary literature, but it seems very likely now, in the mid-sixties, that the period between, say, 1950 and the present will be seen by literary critics of the future as a period of extremely interesting, possibly great, drama. Indeed, it seems possible that today we are witnessing just the beginnings of a renaissance of drama. Critics of the future will be able to see quite clearly what is not generally realized today, that the drama of the last fifteen years or so owes a considerable debt to dramatic techniques and theories first employed and formulated in that immensely fruitful period of dramatic activity, the last twenty years of the Nineteenth Century. These techniques and theories have been developed by the successors of Ibsen, Strindberg and Chekhov, but undoubtedly there are significant traces of these writers' influence in the work of today's dramatists. The main purpose of this collection of extracts from the drama of the last eighty years is to show some of these lines of influence and development.

Knowledge of the influences which have helped to mould contemporary drama does not, of course, involve a lowering of our opinion of its intrinsic merit. It does, however, help to show how pervasive a thing literary tradition is, how any writer, however great and 'original', must draw a great deal of his inspiration not from purely personal sources but from a combination of personal vision and critical awareness of what others have done. Thus, to say that contemporary drama could not exist without the influence of the great dramatists of the late Nineteenth Century is neither to dismiss the dramatists of today as plagiarists nor to view their predecessors as relatively crude precursors. Aeschylus is no less great a dramatist for having, in a sense, prepared the way for Sophocles and Euripides. Drama is constantly striving to understand and interpret its age and the effort is a continuous one, no contribution to the effort being made obsolete by what follows. Strindberg, Ibsen, Chekhov and their successors are a vital part of a particular literary tradition, one which is nourishing the best of today's dramatists. They made as decisive a break with what had gone before as it is possible for any writer to make and in so doing they opened up a range of possibilities which is still being explored today. If one is to speak of a modern dramatic revolution one must locate it in the late Nineteenth Century rather than in the present age.

The charting of the influences which have contributed to contemporary drama can not, of course, be done in purely literary terms, for drama is, above all, an art of *social* ritual, participation and interpretation; great drama speaks to man both as Everyman and as a citizen of a particular age. To understand fully an age's drama, one must be aware of the ideas which were current in that age. Two great dramatists, whose achievements happen almost to define the boundaries of our period, have emphasized very clearly this social aspect of drama. Ibsen spoke of the dramatist's task in the following terms:

> to make clear to himself and thereby to others, the temporal and eternal questions which are astir in the age and in the community to which he belongs.

Again, Brecht, writing in 1940, saw drama as having 'a practical end — to try to discover the best way for people to live together'. Brecht and Ibsen made their social purpose more obvious than the other dramatists of the period, but this social element is present in all drama, even the least didactic, to a certain extent.

A useful starting point for a consideration of the development of modern drama is the conflict between Realism and Naturalism which had its origins in the work of Ibsen and Strindberg. This conflict is still reflected in the division in contemporary drama between 'social' drama and the drama of 'the absurd', as it is now called. HENRIK IBSEN (1828–1906) was the inspiration of a school of dramatic 'Realism' whose adherents saw drama as essentially an investigation and exposure of human and social injustice, hypocrisy and cruelty. Inevitably, since most of Ibsen's followers lacked even a trace of his genius, many of the realistic plays of the period were tedious and prolix examinations of social problems rather than literary achievements. Most of Ibsen's disciples imitated his surface manner without realizing that, far from being merely realistic social criticism, his plays centre on his profound realization of man's tragic addiction to superficial, glib and complacent attitudes. The gap between truth and self-delusion is at the heart of his plays; the concern with contemporary social questions is his starting point, not his goal. Indeed he rejected very succinctly the notion that the chief purpose of his plays was the simple presentation of vice and corruption in a comment on the realistic novelist Zola: 'Zola goes to bathe in the sewer. I go to cleanse it'. Ibsen's immediate influence was immense, and he was a great dramatist by any standards, but the subsequent development of modern drama shows clearly that dramatic Realism was a less fruitful innovation than Naturalism.

Indeed the work of AUGUST STRINDBERG (1849–1912) is the source of much that is often acclaimed as new and revolutionary in contemporary drama: the detailed rendering of the convolutions of human thought in moments of extreme anguish; the absence of obvious motives for action and of traditional methods of character-ization; above all, the presentation of characters and situations not as symbols and configurations of some social 'theme' but simply for their intrinsic interest. The name which Strindberg gave to the movement he inspired was 'Naturalism', a name which, in its insistence on the 'anti-literary' qualities of this new drama, is more meaningful than such tags usually are. Like many of his successors, Strindberg was a cogent and provocative theorist as well as a practising dramatist. This extract from *On Modern Drama and Modern Theatre* of 1889 indicates something of the influence he was to have on such dramatists as, for example, Ionesco and Pinter:

> By means of a table and two chairs one could present the most power-ful conflicts life has to offer; and in this type of art all the discoveries of modern psychology could for the first time be applied in popularized form.

This rejection of the trappings of elaborate productions, and the assertion of the relevance of the new psychology to drama show how closely connected were technique and subject matter in the theatre of Naturalism.

The third of the great dramatic innovators of the late Nineteenth Century, ANTON CHEKHOV (1860–1904), was himself an ardent admirer of Strindberg's work. Chekhov's plays are distinguished from Strindberg's, however, by a characteristically Russian respect, almost reverence, for the virtues of quiet, quotidian, ordinary life. This explains the impatience which he frequently expressed for the drama of social diagnosis and hectic external action. His is the supreme drama of spiritual crystallization; in his plays a meaning emerges almost imperceptibly, for both the characters and the audience, without any obtrusive moral-pointing. It is a mistake, however, to think of Chekhov as a less radical innovator than Ibsen or Strindberg because his views are stated less forcefully. He believed very strongly that the dramatist should preserve a judicial impartiality in his presentation of characters and situations, and should avoid didacticism at all costs. In reply to a comment that his personal views did not emerge from his plays, he said in 1888:

> You are right to require a conscious attitude from the artist towards his work but you mix up two ideas: the solution of the problem and the correct presentation of the problem. Only the latter is obligatory for the artist.

Chekhov's plays demand a very intense, though undemonstrative, style of acting. It is significant that Stanislawski, the founder of a new 'method' of intense and introspective acting, was a young member of the Moscow Art Theatre in the period when several of Chekhov's plays received their first performances there. In our own age the National Theatre production of *Uncle Vanya* has shown the immense possibilities of the Chekhovian theatre.

It has already been said that Ibsen's influence was more immediate than that of Strindberg or Chekhov, and the work of GEORGE BERNARD SHAW (1856–1950) illustrates very well the impact which Ibsen made on his age. Today Shaw is best remembered, perhaps, for the wit of his dialogue and the polemical power of his work, but in his own day his achievement was considered radically original. This is not difficult to understand for his plays impinged on the British theatre of the Nineties, which had become almost incredibly narrow, trivial and predictable. In his early reviews Shaw mounted many scathing attacks on the prevailing conventions:

> The active, germinating life in the households of today cannot be typified by an aristocratic hero, an ingenuous heroine, a gentleman-forger abetted by an Artful Dodger, and a parlormaid, who takes half-sovereigns and kisses from the male visitors.

This was written in November, 1896, in a review of Ibsen's *Little Eyolf* which contains a very unfavourable comparison of the contemporary British theatre with the theatre of Ibsen. The plea is typical of the literary revolutionary: to align art and life once more; to stop considering art as a mere amusing plaything. Shaw himself frequently expressed his debt to Ibsen as the dramatist who had provided an outlet for his creative impulse. Although it would be grossly unfair to dismiss him as a mere imitator of Ibsen, his plays, lacking the organizing principle of a central vision, too often fall back on abstract ideas and polemics. His output, of course, was vast, but modern critical opinion increasingly sees *Saint Joan* as his greatest achievement. Even in this play the 'debate element' occasionally obtrudes — in the discussion of Nationalism and Protestantism, for example — but this shortcoming is more than balanced by the moving exploration of Joan's gradual realization that she is helpless before the sophistry of the public world. Certainly Shaw dominated the English theatre for over thirty years, until his death in 1950.

In fact, it is to Ireland that one must turn for significant British drama in the first half of this century. A key figure in the resurgence of Irish drama which centred on the Abbey Theatre was JOHN MILLINGTON SYNGE (1871–1909). When first produced, his plays, particularly *The Playboy of the Western World* of 1907, received very hostile treatment which disgusted those who appreciated his originality, particularly Lady Gregory and W. B. Yeats. Synge's work is characterized by the beautifully controlled irony which he brought to bear on Ireland. Like Joyce, shortly after him, he was an Irishman who had seen Europe and who was subsequently both attracted and repelled by Irish simplicity and ignorance. In his plays, he drew heavily on the speech rhythms and dialects of Ireland, but used these to express a radical criticism of Irish life. Yeats spoke of Ireland as a land where 'personifications have taken the place of life', and he had Ireland particularly in mind when he defined the social function of literature thus:

> literature, which is a part of that charity that is the forgiveness of sins, will make us understand men however little they conform to our expectations. We will be more interested in heroic men than in heroic actions, and will have a little distrust for everything that can be called good or bad in itself with a very confident heart.

Such views are very close to those expressed in *The Playboy of the Western World*.

Also connected with the Abbey Theatre was SEAN O'CASEY (1884–1964), whose plays, though in many respects similar to Synge's, are much more specifically *political* criticisms of the Irish tendency to obscure every issue with irrelevant sentiment, generalizations and clichés. Several of his plays depict the working class urban Irish fighting for their personal and political freedom, though constantly distracted by animosity and laziness. O'Casey's plays are not just about Ireland, however, for his sense of the waste of human goodness caused by the blind Irish trust in empty political rhetoric, for example, makes his plays genuinely tragic. The characters of Mary of *Juno and the Paycock* (1924) and Norah of *The Plough and the Stars* (1926), for example, are presented with accuracy and passion which are reminiscent of Strindberg.

These Irish dramatists consolidated the achievements of Ibsen, Strindberg and Chekhov and their plays have had a considerable influence on such dramatists as Arnold Wesker who have begun to write since 1950, for they manage to combine a passionate social concern with real dramatic intensity.

Between these Irish dramatists and the contemporary theatre, however, lies one of the greatest literary achievements of this century, the work of BERT BRECHT (1898–1956). Until quite recently, Brecht was better known in this country for his 'anti-Aristotelian' theories of 'epic' theatre than for his actual plays. Even now there is radical disagreement as to his greatness. Like Chekhov's, Brecht's plays must be very well performed if they are not to seem wooden and unduly stylized, and, again like Chekhov, Brecht found a group of actors who could perform his plays as he wanted them performed, the Berliner Ensemble. Here, of course, all similarity between Brecht and Chekhov ends. Brecht frequently proposed solutions for the social situations he dramatized, whereas Chekhov simply presented his situations, leaving any relevant inferences to be drawn by the audience. Brecht saw the theatre not just as 'a temple of the emotions' but as a place where particular human tragedies could be shown, and solutions suggested. He objected to the classical theatre because, he said, it portrayed the human condition as unchanging and unchangeable and he claimed to be inaugurating the theatre of the scientific age, in which problems could be understood and consequently solved:

> man can no longer be described to man as a mere victim, the object of an unknown, but unalterable environment . . . The world of today can be described to the human beings of today only as a world that can be changed.

One's acceptance or rejection of his theories should not, of course, colour one's judgment of the plays. His basic dramatic theme is the vulnerability of goodness in a world of grasping, unscrupulous, plausible evil. He suggests that this vulnerability can be averted by a recognition of the fact that in the present world goodness must be prepared to fight evil on its own terms rather than passively accept victimization. Azdak of *The Caucasian Chalk Circle* (1944–1945) and Shui Ta of *The Good Woman of Setzuan* (1938–1941) represent the element of shrewd remorselessness which aligns itself with innocent and vulnerable goodness. The theme is in some ways very similar to that which Blake presents in *Songs of Innocence and of Experience*.

Apart from Brecht, the modern dramatist who has succeeded most notably in producing a social drama which avoids the danger of shrill didacticism is ARTHUR MILLER (*b*. 1916). Though they have a very definite social point, most of his plays centre on an intense personal tragedy, which is tellingly related to its social setting. Perhaps the influence of Greek drama on his work has helped to save his plays from the assertive didacticism which can so easily mar a social play. Thus, the tragedy of Willie Loman in *Death of a Salesman* (1949) is both the personal tragedy of a man whose life has been based on self-delusion, and a social tragedy in that his death is partly caused and precipitated by the pressures of a cynical and impersonal business world. Like Brecht, Miller has explicitly rejected the idea of the theatre as a place where the audience can simply luxuriate in emotion: 'The end of drama is the creation of higher consciousness and not merely a subjective attack upon the audience's nerves and feelings.' The word 'merely' indicates Miller's low opinion of drama which lacks a social purpose and significance.

In England, one dramatist who has succeeded in writing a social drama which reconciles moving exploration of credible human situations with a desire to convey a social 'message' is ARNOLD WESKER (*b*. 1932). He has said that his work is concerned with the tragic waste caused by philistinism and indifference. As in the case of Brecht, however, Wesker is too often discussed in terms of his political and literary theories rather than as a dramatist. These theories are, of course, relevant to an understanding of his work but they are much less important than the actual plays. In *Roots*, one play from a trilogy which deals with the fortunes over a period of some twenty years of the Kahn family, and of Ronnie Kahn in particular, Wesker takes for his subject a situation rather similar to that of O'Casey's *Juno and the Paycock*, though his treatment of it is very different from O'Casey's. A girl from a working class background is disappointed in her love for a man who she had hoped would remove her from a life with which she is increasingly dissatisfied. In Wesker's play the girl learns a great deal both about herself and her family from her disappointment, and the speech in which she gropes towards these new insights is a fine piece of dramatic writing by any standards. Although parts of the trilogy tend to lack the tension and conflict which are essential to drama, Wesker has progressed further towards the difficult reconciliation of social purpose and the exploration of personal relationships than most of his contemporaries.

The account of modern drama given up to this point might suggest that by far the most influential of the three dramatists whom we considered at the outset was Ibsen. Indeed, until ten years ago such a judgement would have been generally accepted. Until then, with the exception of Luigi Pirandello, the great majority of modern dramatists had been concerned with exploring the possibilities of social realism. Only Pirandello had touched on the themes which are being explored today by the dramatists of the Theatre of the Absurd: such themes as man's infinite capacity for self-delusion, his refusal to accept things as they are and the frequent flights from reality which he resorts to when reality asserts itself. It is Pirandello who provides the only link between Strindberg and Chekhov and today's dramatists of the Absurd.

The dramatists of the first half of this century had been so obsessed with social realism that SAMUEL BECKETT (*b*. 1906), the most prominent of today's dramatists of the Absurd, seems to have turned for many of his themes to the novels of Proust and Joyce, among others. He was, indeed, a disciple of Joyce in Paris. Although his debt to Strindberg and Chekhov is considerable in such matters as the creation of menacing atmospheres in his plays and the rejection of elaborate plots and traditional characterization, he saw that the novels of Joyce had come to grips with the new insights of Twentieth Century philosophy and psychology much more profitably than had Twentieth Century drama. And it is worth remembering that Beckett is a prolific novelist as well as a dramatist. In his plays Beckett sees man as a pathetic creature maintaining a precarious foothold on sanity only by constant evasion and self-delusion. In Beckett's plays, as in Eliot, 'human kind cannot bear very much reality'. Since 1956, Beckett has gradually gained recognition in this country and thus prepared the way for the acceptance of other dramatists who are concerned with rather similar themes.

The best-known of these dramatists is EUGENE IONESCO (*b.* 1912). Ionesco is a less obviously 'difficult' dramatist than Beckett in that he makes his themes fairly obvious, constructs his plays with exact symmetry, and adopts a less stark, more exuberant, approach to characterization than Beckett. Some people consider that Ionesco's characters are more satisfactory, because more positive, vehicles through which to express a sense of the absurdity of life than Beckett's listless creatures. Certainly there is much to be said for the view that Ionesco's most famous character, Berenger, is a successful embodiment of the only kind of tragic vision possible in our age. Ionesco's theme is the difficulty of communication, a difficulty produced not by the deficiencies of human language but by the stagnation of the inner life which can alone, when vigorous and healthy, make words meaningful, more than verbal formulae. He presents this theme through a drama of distorted but still uncomfortably recognizable human figures. In his world the necessity for personal decisions and the importance of simple fundamental emotions are submerged beneath a welter of words, specious logic and a fear of personal commitment. A very interesting feature of modern literary controversy is Ionesco's repugnance for the theatre of Brecht; it is very similar to that of Strindberg for Ibsen's plays. In *Discovering the Theatre*, Ionesco made his position very clear: 'Realism, whether it be socialist or not, falls short of reality, . . . Truth is in our dreams, in the Imagination.' Here, in a cogent and telling paradox, Ionesco dismisses as misguided the social dramatist's attempt to present the 'real' world.

In England, HAROLD PINTER (*b.* 1930) has adapted the themes and techniques of Ionesco and Beckett very successfully. In *The Caretaker* (1959) he creates with considerable wit, deftness and dramatic skill a cluttered microcosm which reflects the mental confusion and aimlessness of three characters who find themselves thrown together in one room. Though physically close, they avoid for the most part real communication, taking refuge in the fatuous and the mundane. This situation gives rise to several extremely funny verbal exchanges as well as to some moments of terror when one character attempts to communicate the things that really matter to him. In Pinter, man is unwilling, rather than unable, to communicate with his fellows.

These, then, are the twelve dramatists from whose work extracts have been chosen. They have been chosen because their work is both representative of modern developments in drama, and of great intrinsic literary worth. Inevitably several good dramatists have not been mentioned, but this is, after all, simply an introduction to a very rich area of modern literature. All the dramatists represented here, and all the extracts, show the ability, indispensable to the dramatist, of rendering fundamental human conflict through a convincing mastery of the subtleties and nuances of speech. This has been the constant criterion. Yeats's definition of drama indicates very well what these dramatists have achieved:

> [drama is] an activity of the souls of the characters, it is an energy, an eddy of life purified of everything but itself.

THE BEGINNINGS OF
MODERN DRAMA

HENRIK IBSEN

Ghosts

THE achievement of Ibsen is the vital starting point for a consideration of the development of modern drama. Although he is today,
perhaps, no longer a major influence, this is simply because his
lessons were fully assimilated by such dramatists as Shaw and
O'Casey. When trying to assess the influence of Ibsen on modern
literature, it is important to remember how highly the young James
Joyce, for example, thought of him. His plays and theories are a
vital part of the Twentieth Century dramatic tradition, constant
sources for the perennial debate as to what drama's aims should be.
The prevailing temper of European drama before Ibsen is the clearest
proof of the originality of his genius. The Romantic Movement had
been essentially lyrical and epic in its ambitions, rather than dramatic, and the post-Romantic period had produced nothing but the
re-working of Shakespeare's plays and the kind of domestic comedy
or melodramatic and turgid 'tragedy' which Shaw, in England, so
memorably attacked.

In *Ghosts* (1881), Ibsen explicitly attacked many of the previously
unquestioned standards by which Europe had lived for perhaps
forty years: the concept of 'duty' (one thinks of *Little Dorrit*); the
unswerving adherence to the tenets of conventional religion as a
comprehensive guide to morals and ethics; the rigid suppression of
any truth which smacked of the scandalous or unsavoury. Ibsen saw
such standards as the 'ghosts' which haunted contemporary society
and frustrated the 'joy of life' which he set over against them. Mrs

Alving describes these 'ghosts' to Pastor Manders in these terms: 'It's all sorts of dead ideas, and lifeless old beliefs, and so forth. They have no vitality, but they cling to us all the same, and we can't get rid of them.' To this the Pastor replies: 'Ah! here we have the fruits of your reading! And pretty fruits they are, upon my word! Oh! those horrible, revolutionary, free-thinking books!' The play is concerned with the tragically unsuccessful struggle of Mrs Alving and her son, Oswald, to escape these ghosts.

In the early episodes we are shown the uneasy relationship between the rather speciously 'progressive' Mrs Alving and the pompous, sanctimonious Pastor Manders. Mrs Alving has financed the building of a new orphange which is to be named after her late husband, the revered Captain Alving. As a result of their deliberations, they decide that to insure the building would be to question the benevolence of God: an example of typically Ibsenite irony. Mrs Alving's son, Oswald, an artist, has returned from Paris for the occasion and immediately forms an attachment to the maid, Regina, the supposed daughter of the carpenter, Engstrand. Meanwhile, Mrs Alving is provoked by Manders to tell him the shocking truth, that her late husband had been utterly dissolute and feckless. Mrs Alving is shocked in her turn by the relevation which Oswald makes to her that he has hereditary syphilis, and that he is subject to fits of disabling insanity. Oswald tells her, further, that he intends to marry Regina, who will look after him, and this forces Mrs Alving to tell her son that Regina is in fact his natural sister, his father's illegitimate daughter by a former maid. Engstrand has been bribed to pretend to be her father. Now the uninsured orphanage burns down and the naïve Manders is tricked by Engstrand into believing himself responsible through negligence, and bribes Engstrand to remain silent. Regina now leaves, and the desolate Mrs Alving and Oswald are left alone together. Oswald gives his mother the duty of administering to him a fatal dose of morphia if he is overtaken by another fit of madness. The play ends as Mrs Alving is faced with this task, Oswald in his madness crying out for 'The sun. The sun'.

The play, then, is clearly about the conflict between 'truth' and 'ghosts'. Only through the truth can the 'joy of life' be attained.

Ibsen's intention in the play is overtly didactic for he makes these points clear several times in the play. Yet the play is much more than a piece of social criticism. In spite of the fact that the play is obviously a vehicle for the revelation of the truth as Ibsen saw it, this social aim does not prevent the character of Mrs Alving from being genuinely tragic in her gradual emotional realization, at a personal level, of the truth of those beliefs about 'ghosts' which she shallowly professed at the beginning of the play. Thus Ibsen succeeded in reconciling his social aim and the exigencies of the tragic form in a manner that eluded many of his successors. One might remark, finally, that Ibsen was generally misunderstood by contemporary audiences, who failed to see, for example, that syphilis is mentioned in the play as a symbol of inherited conventions, and with no desire to 'shock'. Shaw's struggle to have Ibsen's genius recognized in England was a long and hard one.

*   *   *   *   *

The episode which follows occurs at the end of Act One. Oswald has just left, after shocking Manders with the enunciation of his liberal views on morality. Here we see the early stages of the clash between Mrs Alving and conventional morality, as represented by Pastor Manders.

Extract from *Ghosts*

Archer translation.

(*Ibsen's Prose Dramas*, Vol. 2, pp. 36–46.)

OSWALD: . . . Excuse me, Pastor; I know you can't take my point
of view; but I couldn't help speaking out.

[*He goes out through the second door to the right.*]

MRS ALVING: My poor boy!

MANDERS: You may well say so. Then that's what he has come to!

[MRS ALVING *looks at him silently.*]

MANDERS [*walking up and down*]: He called himself the Prodigal
Son — alas! alas!

[MRS ALVING *continues looking at him.*]

MANDERS: And what do you say to all this?

MRS ALVING: I say that Oswald was right in every word.

MANDERS [*stands still*]: Right! Right! In such principles?

MRS ALVING: Here, in my loneliness, I have come to the same way
of thinking, Pastor Manders. But I've never dared to say anything.
Well! now my boy shall speak for me.

MANDERS: You are much to be pitied, Mrs Alving. But now I must
speak seriously to you. And now it is no longer your business
manager and adviser, your own and your late husband's early
friend, who stands before you. It is the priest — the priest who
stood before you in the moment of your life when you had gone
most astray.

MRS ALVING: And what has the priest to say to me?

MANDERS: I will first stir up your memory a little. The time is well
chosen. Tomorrow will be the tenth anniversary of your husband's
death. Tomorrow the memorial in his honour will be unveiled.
Tomorrow I shall have to speak to the whole assembled multitude.
But today I will speak to you alone.

MRS ALVING: Very well, Pastor Manders. Speak.

MANDERS: Do you remember that after less than a year of married
life you stood on the verge of an abyss? That you forsook your
house and home? That you fled from your husband? Yes, Mrs

Alving — fled, fled, and refused to return to him, however much he begged and prayed you?

MRS ALVING: Have you forgotten how infinitely miserable I was in that first year?

MANDERS: It is only the spirit of rebellion that craves for happiness in this life. What right have we human beings to happiness? No, we have to do our duty! And your duty was to hold firmly to the man you had once chosen and to whom you were bound by a holy tie.

MRS ALVING: You know very well what sort of life Alving was leading — what excesses he was guilty of.

MANDERS: I know very well what rumours there were about him, and I am the last to approve the life he led in his young day, if report did not wrong him. But a wife is not to be her husband's judge. It was your duty to bear with humility the cross which a Higher Power had, for your own good, laid upon you. But instead of that you rebelliously throw away the cross, desert the backslider whom you should have supported, go and risk your good name and reputation, and—nearly succeed in ruining other people's reputation into the bargain.

MRS ALVING: Other people's? One other person's, you mean.

MANDERS: It was incredibly reckless of you to seek refuge with me.

MRS ALVING: With our clergyman? With our intimate friend?

MANDERS: Just on that account. Yes, you may thank God that I possessed the necessary firmness; that I dissuaded you from your wild designs; and that it was vouchsafed me to lead you back to the path of duty, and home to your lawful husband.

MRS ALVING: Yes, Pastor Manders, it was certainly your work.

MANDERS: I was but a poor instrument in a Higher Hand. And what a blessing has it not been to you, all the days of your life, that I got you to resume the yoke of duty and obedience! Did not everything happen as I foretold? Did not Alving turn his back on his errors, as a man should? Did he not live with you from that time, lovingly and blamelessly, all his days? Did he not become a benefactor to the whole district? And did he not raise you up to him, so that you little by little became his assistant in all his undertakings? And a capital assistant, too—Oh! I know, Mrs Alving, that praise is due to you. But now I come to the next great error in your life.

MRS ALVING: What do you mean?

MANDERS: Just as you once disowned a wife's duty, so you have since disowned a mother's.

MRS ALVING: Ah!

MANDERS: You have been all your life under the dominion of a pestilent spirit of self-will. All your efforts have been bent towards emancipation and lawlessness. You have never known how to endure any bond. Everything that has weighed upon you in life you have cast away without care or conscience, like a burden you could throw off at will. It did not please you to be a wife any longer, and you left your husband. You found it troublesome to be a mother, and you sent your child forth among strangers.

MRS ALVING: Yes. That is true. I did so.

MANDERS: And thus you have become a stranger to him.

MRS ALVING: No! no! I am not.

MANDERS: Yes, you are; you must be. And how have you got him back again? Bethink yourself well, Mrs Alving. You have sinned greatly against your husband;—that you recognize by raising yonder memorial to him. Recognize now, also, how you have sinned against your son. There may be time to lead him back from the paths of error. Turn back yourself, and save what may yet be saved in him. For [*with uplifted finger*] verily, Mrs Alving, you are a guilt-laden mother!—This I have thought it my duty to say to you. [*Silence.*]

MRS ALVING [*slowly and with self-control*]: You have now spoken out, Pastor Manders; and tomorrow you are to speak publicly in memory of my husband. I shall not speak tomorrow. But now I will speak frankly to you, as you have spoken to me.

MANDERS: To be sure; you will plead excuses for your conduct —

MRS ALVING: No. I will only narrate.

MANDERS: Well?

MRS ALVING: All that you have just said about me and my husband and our life after you had brought me back to the path of duty —

as you called it — about all that you know nothing from personal observation. From that moment you, who had been our intimate friend, never set foot in our house again.

MANDERS: You and your husband left the town immediately after.

MRS ALVING: Yes; and in my husband's lifetime you never came to see us. It was business that forced you to visit me when you undertook the affairs of the Orphanage.

MANDERS [*softly and uncertainly*]: Helen — if that is meant as a reproach, I would beg you to bear in mind —

MRS ALVING: — the regard you owed to your position, yes; and that I was a runaway wife. One can never be too careful with such unprincipled creatures.

MANDERS: My dear — Mrs Alving, you know that is an absurd exaggeration.

MRS ALVING: Well, well, suppose it is. My point is that your judgment as to my married life is founded upon nothing but current gossip.

MANDERS: Well, I admit that. What then?

MRS ALVING: Well, then, Mr Manders — I will tell you the truth. I have sworn to myself that one day you should know it — you alone!

MANDERS: What is the truth, then?

MRS ALVING: The truth is that my husband died just as dissolute as he had lived all his days.

MANDERS [*feeling after a chair*]: What do you say?

MRS ALVING: After nineteen years of marriage, as dissolute — in his desires at any rate — as he was before you married us.

MANDERS: And those — those wild oats, those irregularities, those excessess, if you like, you call a 'dissolute life'?

MRS ALVING: Our doctor used the expression.

MANDERS: I don't understand you.

MRS ALVING: You need not.

MANDERS: It almost makes me dizzy. Your whole married life, the seeming union of all these years, was nothing more than a hidden abyss!

MRS ALVING: Nothing more. Now you know it.

MANDERS: This is — it will take me long to accustom myself to the thought. I can't grasp it! I can't realise it! But how was it possible to — ? How could such a state of things be kept dark?

MRS ALVING: That has been my ceaseless struggle, day after day. After Oswald's birth, I thought Alving seemed to be a little better. But it didn't last long. And then I had to struggle twice as hard, fighting for life or death, so that nobody should know what sort of man my child's father was. And you know what power Alving had of winning people's hearts. Nobody seemed able to believe anything but good of him. He was one of those people whose life does not bite upon their reputation. But at last, Mr Manders — for you must know the whole story — the most repulsive thing of all happened.

MANDERS: More repulsive than the rest?

MRS ALVING: I had gone on bearing with him, although I knew very well the secrets of his life out of doors. But when he brought the scandal within our own walls —

MANDERS: Impossible! Here!

MRS ALVING: Yes; here in our own home. It was there [*pointing towards the first door on the right*], in the dining-room, that I first got to know of it. I was busy with something in there, and the door was standing ajar. I heard our housemaid come up from the garden, with water for those flowers.

MANDERS: Well — ?

MRS ALVING: Soon after I heard Alving come too. I heard him say something softly to her. And then I heard — [*with a short laugh*] — oh! it still sounds in my ears, so hateful and yet so ludicrous — I heard my own servant-maid whisper, 'Let me go, Mr Alving! Let me be.'

MANDERS: What unseemly levity on his part! But it cannot have been more than levity, Mrs Alving; believe me, it cannot.

MRS ALVING: I soon knew what to believe. Mr Alving had his way with the girl; and that connection had consequences, Mr Manders.

MANDERS [*as though petrified*]: Such things in this house! in this house!

MRS ALVING: I had borne a great deal in this house. To keep him at home in the evenings — and at night — I had to make myself his boon companion in his secret orgies up in his room. There I have had to sit alone with him, to clink glasses and drink with him, and to listen to his ribald, silly talk. I have had to fight with him to get him dragged to bed —

MANDERS [*moved*]: And you were able to bear all that?

MRS ALVING: I had to bear it for my little boy's sake. But when the last insult was added; when my own servant-maid — Then I swore to myself: This shall come to an end. And so I took the reins into my own hands — the whole control over him and everything else. For now I had a weapon against him, you see; he dared not oppose me. It was then I sent Oswald from home. He was in his seventh year, and was beginning to observe and ask questions, as children do. That I could not bear. It seemed to me the child must be poisoned by merely breathing the air of this polluted home. That was why I sent him away. And now you can see, too, why he was never allowed to set foot inside his home so long as his father lived. No one knows what it has cost me.

MANDERS: You have indeed had a life of trial.

MRS ALVING: I could never have borne it if I hadn't had my work. For I may truly say that I have worked! All those additions to the estate — all the improvements — all the useful appliances, that won Alving such general praise — do you suppose *he* had energy for anything of the sort? — he who lay all day on the sofa and read an old court guide! No; this I will tell you too; it was I who urged him on when he had his better intervals; it was I who had to drag the whole load when he relapsed into his evil ways, or sank into querulous wretchedness.

MANDERS: And to that man you raise a memorial?

MRS ALVING: There you see the power of an evil conscience.

MANDERS: Evil — ? What do you mean?

MRS ALVING: It always seemed to me impossible but that the truth must come out and be believed. So the Asylum was to deaden all rumours and banish doubt.

B

MANDERS: In that you have certainly not missed your aim, Mrs Alving.

MRS ALVING: And besides, I had one other reason. I did not wish that Oswald, my own boy, should inherit anything whatever from his father.

MANDERS: Then it is Alving's fortune that — ?

MRS ALVING: Yes. The sums I have spent upon the Orphanage, year by year, make up the amount — I have reckoned it up precisely — the amount which made Lieutenant Alving a good match in his day.

MANDERS: I don't quite understand —

MRS ALVING: It was my purchase-money. I do not choose that that money should pass into Oswald's hands. My son shall have everything from me — everything. [OSWALD *enters through the second door to the right; he has taken off his hat and overcoat in the hall.* MRS ALVING *goes towards him.*] Are you back again already? My dear, dear boy!

OSWALD: Yes. What can a fellow do out of doors in this eternal rain? But I hear dinner's ready. That's capital!

REGINA [*with a parcel, from the dining-room*]: A parcel has come for you, Mrs Alving. [*Hands it to her.*]

MRS ALVING [*with a glance at* MR MANDERS]: No doubt copies of the ode for tomorrow's ceremony.

MANDERS: Hm —

REGINA: And dinner is ready.

MRS ALVING: Very well. We'll come directly. I'll just — [*Begins to open the parcel.*]

REGINA [*to Oswald*]: Would Mr Alving like red or white wine?

OSWALD: Both, if you please.

REGINA: Bien. Very well, sir. [*She goes into the dining-room*].

OSWALD: I may as well help to uncork it. [*He also goes into the dining-room, the door of which swings half open behind him.*]

MRS ALVING [*who has opened the parcel*]: Yes, as I thought. Here is the Ceremonial Ode, Pastor Manders.

MANDERS [*with folded hands*]: With what countenance I'm to deliver my discourse tomorrow — !

MRS ALVING: Oh! you'll get through it somehow.

MANDERS: Yes; it would not do to provoke scandal.

MRS ALVING [*under her breath, but firmly*]: No. But then this long, hateful comedy will be ended. From the day after tomorrow it shall be for me as though he who is dead had never lived in this house. No one shall be here but my boy and his mother. [*From within the dining-room comes the noise of a chair overturned, and at the same moment is heard*]:

REGINA [*sharply but whispering*]: Oswald! take care! are you mad? Let me go!

MRS ALVING [*starts in terror*]: Ah!

[*She stares wildly towards the half-opened door.* OSWALD *is heard coughing and humming. A bottle is uncorked.*]

MANDERS [*excited*]: What in the world is the matter? What is it, Mrs Alving?

MRS ALVING [*hoarsely*]: Ghosts! The couple from the conservatory — risen again!

MANDERS: What! Is it possible! Regina — ? Is she — ?

MRS ALVING: Yes, Come. Not another word!

[*She seizes Mr Manders by the arm and walks unsteadily towards the dining-room.*]

QUESTIONS AND DISCUSSION POINTS

1. Ibsen is obviously concerned at this early stage of the play with the exposition of necessary background to the story. How does he manage to make this exposition dramatically effective?

2. What do you think Ibsen's attitude towards Mrs Alving is?

3. Consider Ibsen's use of irony in this episode.

4. What do you consider the most dramatically effective moment in this episode?

5. Does Ibsen succeed in enlisting any degree of sympathy in us for Pastor Manders?

6. What prevents this episode from lapsing into a mere argument or debate?

AUGUST STRINDBERG

Miss Julie

IN A preface to *Miss Julie* (1888), Strindberg issued his first and most famous challenge to the prevailing dramatic traditions of Europe: 'When we have grown strong as the pioneers of the French Revolution, we shall be happy and relieved to see the national parks cleared of ancient rotting trees which have stood too long in the way of others equally entitled to a period of growth — as relieved as we are when an incurable invalid dies.' The tone of this is characteristically blunt and uncompromising. The aspect of contemporary drama which he most vehemently criticized at this stage in his career was the conventional stereotyped methods of characterization:

> I do not believe, therefore, in simple stage characters; and the summary judgement of authors — this man is stupid, that one brutal, this jealous, that stingy, and so forth — should be challenged by the Naturalists who know the richness of the soul-complex and realize that vice has a reverse side very much like virtue.

Miss Julie is, together with *The Father*, of 1887, a wonderful justification of the claims made in such statements as this. It contains no moral judgements, no obvious motivation and no neat dénouement. The play was first produced in Paris, at the Théâtre Libre, for Strindberg never gained the acclaim he deserved in his native city, Stockholm.

The play has three characters: Miss Julie, the neurotic product of a stormy marriage which she remembers only too well; Jean, a valet in the service of Julie's father, the Count; and Kristin, the cook, whom Jean plans to marry. Julie, in the absence of her father, makes advances towards Jean at the Midsummer Eve festivities on her father's estate. Jean responds by exploiting Julie's sentimentality and naïvety by stories of how he had viewed her from afar as a boy and with promises that he will take her with him to Switzerland where they will run an hotel. The entire action of the play covers less than twenty-four hours and in this time we learn of the hatred of men which Julie has inherited from her mother, and which she feels she is betraying by her relationship with Jean. Julie constantly vacillates between optimism and despair, but the return of her father, who never actually appears on stage, is sufficient to show both Julie and Jean the impossibility of their plans. Julie, however, realizes too the impossibility of returning to her former way of life and as the play ends she walks away with a razor, in an almost hypnotic state, and the lesser characters are left, as at the end of most tragedies, to pursue their routine, having failed to understand the nature and intensity of Julie's aspirations.

The heart of the play is, of course, the clash of wills and temperaments between Julie and Jean. Part of Strindberg's triumph in the play is to make a view of the play as a class conflict almost comically irrelevant. The relationship is something which defies conventional moral categories, a point which Strindberg makes by allowing Kristin to reflect on the events of the main action: 'God help us. I've never known such goings on.' Perhaps his greatest achievement, however, is his rendering of the drifting desires of Julie's mind and heart, the pity which he creates for her, and the wonder at the sheer power of her hopes and aspirations. What Eugene O'Neill said of him is borne out by this play, and his is only one of many such tributes by, for example, O'Casey, Miller, Ionesco, and Cocteau: '[Strindberg is] the precursor of all modernity in our present theatre, just as Ibsen, a lesser man as he himself surmised, was the father of the modernity of twenty years or so ago.' In substance, the tribute is still true today.

The following episode occurs after Jean and Julie have resolved to run away together. Jean's resolution crumbles, however, at the thought of the Count's return, and Julie is increasingly alone. Shortly after this episode comes the rejection of Julie by Jean, and her suicide. It illustrates very well Strindberg's mastery of what was later to be called the 'stream of consciousness' technique, and of dramatic symbolism.

Extract from *Miss Julie*

Elizabeth Sprigge translation, Constable, pp. 105–110.

[*The sun has risen and is shining on the treetops. The light gradually changes until it slants in through the windows.* JEAN *goes to the door and beckons.* JULIE *enters in travelling clothes, carrying a small bird-cage covered with a cloth which she puts on a chair.*]

JULIE: I'm ready.

JEAN: Hush! Kristin's up.

JULIE [*in a very nervous state*]: Does she suspect anything?

JEAN: Not a thing. But, my God, what a sight you are!

JULIE: Sight? What do you mean?

JEAN: You're white as a corpse and — pardon me — your face is dirty.

JULIE: Let me wash then. [*Goes to the sink and washes her face and hands.*] There. Give me a towel. Oh! The sun is rising.

JEAN: And that breaks the spell.

JULIE: Yes, The spell of Midsummer Eve . . . But listen, Jean. Come with me. I've got the money.

JEAN [*sceptically*]: Enough?

JULIE: Enough to start with. Come with me. I can't travel alone today. It's Midsummer Day, remember. I'd be packed into a suffocating train among crowds of people who'd all stare at me. And it would stop at every station while I yearned for wings. No, I can't do that, I simply can't. There will be memories too; memories of Midsummer Days when I was little. The leafy church — birch and lilac — the gaily-spread dinner table, relatives, friends — evening in the park — dancing and music and flowers and fun. Oh, however far you run away — there'll always be memories in the baggage car — and remorse and guilt.

JEAN: I will come with you, but quickly now then, before it's too late. At once.

JULIE: Put on your things. [*Picks up the cage.*]

JEAN: No luggage mind. That would give us away.

JULIE: No, only what we can take with us in the carriage.

30

JEAN [*fetching his hat*]: What on earth have you got there? What is it?

JULIE: Only my greenfinch. I don't want to leave it behind.

JEAN: Well, I'll be damned. We're to take a bird-cage along, are we? You're crazy. Put that cage down.

JULIE: It's the only thing I'm taking from my home. The only living creature who cares for me since Diana [*her dog*] went off like that. Don't be cruel. Let me take it.

JEAN: Put that cage down, I tell you — and don't talk sò loud. Kristin will hear.

JULIE: No, I won't leave it in strange hands. I'd rather you killed it.

JEAN: Give the little beast here then and I'll wring its neck.

JULIE: But don't hurt it, don't . . . no, I can't.

JEAN: Give it here. I can.

JULIE [*taking the bird out of the cage and kissing it*]: Dear little Serena, must you die and leave your mistress?

JEAN: Please don't make a scene. It's *your* life and future we're worrying about. Come on, quick now!
[*He snatches the bird from her, puts it on a board and picks up a chopper.* JULIE *turns away.*]
You should have learnt how to kill chickens instead of target-shooting. Then you wouldn't faint at a drop of blood.

JULIE [*screaming*]: Kill me too! Kill me! You who can butcher an innocent creature without a quiver. Oh, how I hate you, how I loathe you! There is blood between us now. I curse the hour I first saw you. I curse the hour I was conceived in my mother's womb.

JEAN: What's the use of cursing. Let's go.

JULIE [*going to the chopping-block as if drawn against her will*]: No, I won't go yet. I can't . . . I must look. Listen! There's a carriage. [*Listens without taking her eyes off the board and chopper.*] You don't think I can bear the sight of blood. You think I'm so weak. Oh, how I should like to see your blood and your brains on a chopping-block! I'd like to see the whole of your sex swimming like that in a sea of blood. I think I could drink out of your skull, bathe my feet in your broken breast and eat your heart roasted whole. You think I'm weak. You think I love you, that my womb yearned for your seed and I want to carry your offspring under my heart and nourish it with my blood. You think I want to bear your child and take your name. By the way, what is your name? I've never heard your surname. I don't suppose you've got one. I should be 'Mrs. Hovel' or 'Madam Dunghill'. You dog wearing my collar, you lackey with my crest on your buttons! I share you with my cook; I'm my own servant's rival! Oh! Oh! Oh! . . . You think I'm a coward and will run away. No, now I'm going to stay — and let the storm break. My father will come back . . . find his desk broken open . . . his money gone. Then he'll ring that bell — twice for the valet — and then he'll send for the police . . . and I shall tell everything. Everything. Oh how wonderful to make an end of it all — a real end! He has a stroke and dies and that's the end of all of us. Just peace and quietness . . . eternal rest. The coat of arms broken on the coffin and the Count's line extinct . . . But the valet's line goes on in an orphanage, wins laurels in the gutter and ends in jail.

JEAN: There speaks the noble blood! Bravo, Miss Julie. But now, don't let the cat out of the bag.

[KRISTIN *enters dressed for church, carrying a prayerbook.* JULIE *rushes to her and flings herself into her arms for protection.*]

JULIE: Help me Kristin! Protect me from this man!

KRISTIN [*unmoved and cold*]: What goings-on for a feast day morning!

[*Sees the board.*] And what a filthy mess. What's it all about? Why are you screaming and carrying on so?

JULIE: Kristin, you're a woman and my friend. Beware of that scoundrel!

JEAN [*embarrassed*]: While you ladies are talking things over, I'll go and shave. [*Slips into his room.*]

JULIE: You must understand. You must listen to me.

KRISTIN: I certainly don't understand such loose ways. Where are you off to in those travelling clothes? And he had his hat on, didn't he, eh?

JULIE: Listen, Kristin. Listen, I'll tell you everything.

KRISTIN: I don't want to know anything.

JULIE: You must listen.

KRISTIN: What to? Your nonsense with Jean? I don't care a rap about that; it's nothing to do with me. But if you're thinking of getting him to run off with you, we'll soon put a stop to that.

JULIE [*very nervously*]: Please try to be calm, Kristin, and listen. I can't stay here, nor can Jean — so we must go abroad.

KRISTIN: Hm, hm!

JULIE [*brightening*]: But you see, I've had an idea. Supposing we all three go — abroad — to Switzerland and start a hotel together . . . I've got some money, you see . . . and Jean and I could run the whole thing — and I thought you would take charge of the kitchen. Wouldn't that be splendid? Say yes, do. If you come with us everything will be fine. Oh do say yes! [*Puts her arms round* KRISTIN.]

KRISTIN [*coolly thinking*]: Hm, hm.

JULIE [*presto tempo*]: You've never travelled, Kristin. You should go abroad and see the world. You've no idea how nice it is travelling by train — new faces all the time and new countries. On our way through Hamburg we'll go to the zoo — you'll love that — and we'll go to the theatre and the opera too . . . and when we get to Munich there'll be the museums, dear, and pictures by Rubens and Raphael — the great painters, you know . . . You've heard of Munich, haven't you? Where King Ludwig lived — you know, the king who went mad . . . We'll see his castles — some of his castles are still just like in fairy-tales . . . and from there it's not far to Switzerland — and the Alps. Think of the Alps, Kristin dear, covered with snow in the middle of summer . . . and there are oranges there and trees that are green the whole year round . . .

[JEAN *is seen in the door of his room, sharpening his razor on a strop which he holds with his teeth and his left hand. He listens to the talk with satisfaction and now and then nods approval.* JULIE *continues, tempo prestissimo.*]

And then we'll get a hotel . . . and I'll sit at the desk, while Jean receives the guest and goes out marketing and writes letters . . .

There's life for you! Trains whistling, buses driving up, bells ringing upstairs and downstairs ... and I shall make out the bills — and I shall cook them too ... you've no idea how nervous travellers are when it comes to paying their bills. And you — you'll sit like a queen in the kitchen ... of course there won't be any standing at the stove for you. You'll always have to be nicely dressed and ready to be seen, and with your looks — no, I'm not flattering you — one fine day you'll catch yourself a husband ... some rich Englishman, I shouldn't wonder — they're the ones who are easy — [*slowing down*] to catch. And then we'll get rich and build ourselves a villa on Lake Como ... of course it rains there a little now and then — but — [*dully*] — the sun must shine there too sometimes — even though it seems gloomy — and if not — then we can come home again — come back — [*pause*] — here — or somewhere else . . . .

KRISTIN: Look here, Miss Julie, do you believe all that yourself?

JULIE [*exhausted*]: Do I believe it?

KRISTIN: Yes.

JULIE [*wearily*]: I don't know. I don't believe anything any more. [*Sinks down on the bench; her head in her arms on the table.*] Nothing. Nothing at all.

QUESTIONS AND DISCUSSION POINTS

1. 'Because they are modern characters, living in a period of transition more feverishly hysterical than its predecessor at least, I have drawn my figures vacillating, disintegrated, a blend of old and new.' (Preface to *Miss Julie*.) Do Strindberg's characters strike you as being more credible and subtly drawn than Ibsen's? Can you add anything to what Strindberg says here about his method of characterization?

2. Does Strindberg give any hint or guide as to what he thinks our attitude towards his characters should be?

3. What are Miss Julie's strengths and shortcomings as revealed in this scene? Is there any trace here of the misogyny frequently attributed to Strindberg?

4. 'It seems to me that the psychological process is what interests people most today. Our inquisitive souls are no longer satisfied with seeing a thing happen; we must also know how it happens.' (Preface to *Miss Julie*). How successful would you say Strindberg is in showing the actual process of Miss Julie's thoughts?

5. What is the dramatic function of Jean's butchering of the greenfinch?

6. What elements do you think would make such a scene unacceptable to most of its contemporary audiences?

ANTON CHEKHOV

Uncle Vanya

UNCLE VANYA (1897) is a quite eventful play by Chekhovian
standards, including as it does an attempted murder and a planned
suicide. The plot, too, is more complex than in most of Chekhov's
plays, reflecting, perhaps, the fact that the play is a revision of *The
Wood Demon* of 1889 in which Dr Astroff, the visionary medical
man, is the central character. *Uncle Vanya* presents a contrast
between two ways of life, namely the urban, sophisticated and
academic life as represented by Serebrakoff, the retired Moscow
professor, and his wife Helena, and the rural, simple and agricultural
life represented primarily by Vanya and Sonia. Astroff, educated,
politically-minded and gloomily philosophical, occupies a position
midway between these two extremes.

When the play begins, Ivan Voitski (Vanya) and Sonia, Serebrakoff's daughter by a previous marriage, are being visited by
Serebrakoff, whose previous wife was Vanya's sister, and by his
present wife, Helena. Vanya's mother, the widow of a privy
councillor, is immensely proud of Serebrakoff, and indeed he has
been supported in Moscow largely by the profits of the Voitski
farm. The routine of the farm has been completely disrupted by the
visit, a fact which Vanya bemoans: 'Ever since the professor and his
wife have come, our daily life seems to have jumped the track.'
Vanya is in love with Helena, as indeed is Astroff, and Sonia
harbours a secret love for Astroff. Serebrakoff calls a meeting of the
family and announces his decision to sell the farm and invest the

proceeds in bonds, conveniently forgetting that the farm belongs legally to Sonia. This plan enrages the normally placid Vanya to the point of his attempting to murder Serebrakoff, whom he now sees for what he is, a pretentious pedant, a failure even in the academic world. He despairs at the thought of having spent the greater part of his life (he is forty seven) in working to support this man and his absurd pretensions: 'We used to think of you as almost superhuman, but now the scales have fallen from my eyes and I see you as you are. You write on art without knowing anything about it. Those books of yours which I used to admire are not worth one copper copeck. You are a hoax!' Having failed in his attempt to murder Serebrakoff, who is now preparing a hasty departure, Vanya contemplates suicide. Astroff tries to dissuade him from this course, and Vanya turns to him despairingly for some glimmer of hope which might make the future tolerable. Astroff can only launch once more into his Schopenhauerian pessimism which finds no hope in the present situation:

> It may be that posterity, which will despise us for our blind and stupid lives, will find some road to happiness; but we — you and I — have but one hope, the hope that we may be visited by visions, perhaps by pleasant ones, as we lie resting in our graves.

Astroff is clearly found wanting at this moment of spiritual crisis; he takes refuge in conventional attitudes; he cannot help Vanya.

It is through Sonia that Vanya is finally brought to a realization of the intrinsic value of the life he and Sonia have been leading, a value which remains in spite of his disillusionment with Serebrakoff. Thus after the glare and glitter of the Serebrakoffs' visit, after the departure of Astroff, things are as they were except that the way of life that was dedicated formerly to the financial maintenance of a charlatan is now appreciated for its own sake, as a source of spiritual calm and equipoise, as a counterbalance to the essentially restless and unsatisfying life of the Serebrakoffs and Astroff. Thus the play ends with Sonia's vision of future happiness: 'We shall rest.'

Obviously, this is not a play which makes a direct or immediate assault on the audience's emotions. It was, indeed, given a rather luke-warm reception by its early audiences; gradually, however, it was recognized for the masterpiece of subtle psychological exploration of the apparently ordinary and prosaic that it is. Chekhov is a dramatist whose every sentence repays thought, and whose simplest phrases take on symbolic overtones when the tranquil intensity of his art is fully realized.

*   *   *   *   *

The following episode is the end of the play. It illustrates very well Chekhov's ability to allow meaning and emotional power to emerge very gradually.

Extract from *Uncle Vanya* (end of Act IV).

(*Six Famous Plays by Anton Tchekhov*, pp. 236–243. Published by Gerald Duckworth).

VOITSKI: Leave me alone.

ASTROFF [*to* SONIA]: Sonia, your uncle has stolen a bottle of morphine out of my medicine-case and won't give it up. Tell him that his behaviour is — well, unwise. I haven't time, I must be going.

SONIA: Uncle Vanya, did you take the morphine?

ASTROFF: Yes, he took it. [*A pause.*] I am absolutely sure.

SONIA: Give it up! Why do you want to frighten us? [*Tenderly.*] Give it up, Uncle Vanya! My misfortune is perhaps even greater than yours, but I am not plunged in despair. I endure my sorrow, and shall endure it until my life comes to a natural end. You must endure yours, too. [*A pause.*] Give it up! Dear, darling Uncle Vanya. Give it up! [*She weeps.*] You are so good, I am sure you will have pity on us and give it up. You must endure your sorrow. Uncle Vanya; you must endure it.

[VOITSKI *takes a bottle from the drawer of the table and hands it to* ASTROFF].

VOITSKI: There it is! [*To* SONIA]. And now, we must get to work at once; we must do something, or else I shall not be able to endure it.

SONIA: Yes, yes, to work! As soon as we have seen them off we shall go to work. [*She nervously straightens out the papers on the table.*] Everything is in a muddle!

ASTROFF [*putting the bottle in his case, which he straps together*]: Now I can be off.

[HELENA *comes in.*]

HELENA: Are you here, Ivan? We are starting in a moment. Go to Alexander, he wants to speak to you.

SONIA: Go, Uncle Vanya. [*She takes* VOITSKI'S *arm.*] Come, you and papa must make peace; that is absolutely necessary.

[SONIA *and* VOITSKI *go out.*]

39

HELENA: I am going away. [*She gives* ASTROFF *her hand.*] Good-bye.

ASTROFF: So soon?

HELENA: The carriage is waiting.

ASTROFF: Good-bye.

HELENA: You promised me you would go away yourself today.

ASTROFF: I have not forgotten. I am going at once. [*A pause.*] Were you frightened? Was it so terrible?

HELENA: Yes.

ASTROFF: Couldn't you stay? Couldn't you? Tomorrow — in the forest —

HELENA: No. It is all settled, and that is why I can look you so bravely in the face. Our departure is fixed. One thing I must ask of you: don't think too badly of me; I should like you to respect me.

ASTROFF: Ah! [*With an impatient gesture.*] Stay, I implore you! Confess that there is nothing for you to do in this world. You have no object in life; there is nothing to occupy your attention, and sooner or later your feelings must master you. It is inevitable. It would be better if it happened not in Kharkoff or in Kursk, but here, in Nature's lap. It would then at least be poetical, even beautiful. Here you have the forest, the houses half in ruins that Turgenieff writes of.

HELENA: How comical you are! I am angry with you and yet I shall always remember you with pleasure. You are interesting and original. You and I will never meet again, and so I shall tell you — why should I conceal it? — that I am just a little in love with you. Come, one more last pressure of our hands and then let us part good friends. Let us not bear each other any ill will.

ASTROFF [*pressing her hand*]: Yes, go. [*Thoughtfully.*] You seem to be sincere and good, and yet there is something strangely disquieting about all your personality. No sooner did you arrive here with your husband than every one whom you found busy and actively creating something was forced to drop his work and give himself up for the whole summer to your husband's gout and yourself. You and he have infected us with your idleness.

I have been swept off my feet; I have not put my hand to a thing for weeks, during which sickness has been running its course unchecked among the people, and the peasants have been pasturing their cattle in my woods and young plantations. Go where you will, you and your husband will always carry destruction in your train. I am joking of course, and yet I am strangely sure that had you stayed here we should have been overtaken by the most immense desolation. I would have gone to my ruin, and you — you would not have prospered. So go! E finita la commedia!

HELENA [*snatching a pencil off* ASTROFF'S *table, and hiding it with a quick movement*]: I shall take this pencil for memory!

ASTROFF: How strange it is. We meet, and then suddenly it seems that we must part forever. That is the way in this world. As long as we are alone, before Uncle Vanya comes in with a bouquet — allow me — to kiss you good-bye — may I? [*He kisses her on the cheek.*] So! Splendid!

HELENA: I wish you every happiness. [*She glances about her.*] For once in my life, I shall! and scorn the consequences. [*She kisses him impetuously, and they quickly part.*] I must go.

ASTROFF: Yes, go. If the carriage is there, then start at once. [*They stand listening.*]

ASTROFF: E finita!

[VOITSKI, SEREBRAKOFF, MME VOITSKAYA *with her book,* TELEGIN, *and* SONIA *come in.*]

SEREBRAKOFF [*to* VOITSKI]: Shame on him who bears malice for the past. I have gone through so much in the last few hours that I feel capable of writing a whole treatise on the conduct of life for the instruction of posterity. I gladly accept your apology, and myself ask your forgiveness. [*He kisses* VOITSKI *three times.* HELENA *embraces* SONIA.]

VOITSKI: You will regularly receive the same amount as before. Everything will be as before.

SEREBRAKOFF [*kissing* MME VOITSKAYA'S *hand*]: Mother!

MME VOITSKAYA [*kissing him*]: Have your picture taken, Alexander and send me one. You know how dear you are to me.

TELEGIN: Good-bye, your Excellency. Don't forget us.

SEREBRAKOFF [*kissing his daughter*]: Good-bye, good-bye all.
[*Shaking hands with* ASTROFF.] Many thanks for your opinions and your enthusiasm, but let me, as an old man, give one word of advice at parting: do something, my friend! Work! Do something! [*They all bow.*] Good luck to you all.
[*He goes out, followed by* MME VOITSKAYA *and* SONIA.]

VOITSKI [*kissing* HELENA's *hand fervently*]: Good-bye — forgive me. I shall never see you again!

HELENA [*touched*]: Good-bye, dear boy.
[*She lightly kisses his head as he bends over her hand, and goes out.*]

ASTROFF: Tell them to bring my carriage around too, Waffles.

TELEGIN: All right, old man.
[ASTROFF *and* VOITSKI *are left behind alone.* ASTROFF *collects his paints and drawing materials on the table and packs them away in a box.*]

ASTROFF: Why don't you go to see them off?

VOITSKI: Let them go! I – I can't go out there. I feel too sad. I must go to work on something at once. To work! To work!
[*He rummages through his papers on the table. A pause. The tinkling of bells is heard as the horses trot away.*]

ASTROFF: They have gone! The professor, I suppose, is glad to go. He couldn't be tempted back now by a fortune.
[MARINA *comes in.*]

MARINA: They have gone. [*She sits down in an armchair and knits her stocking.*]
[SONIA *comes in wiping her eyes.*]

SONIA: They have gone. God be with them. [*To her uncle.*] And now, Uncle Vanya, let us do something!

VOITSKI: To work! To work!

SONIA: It is long since you and I have sat together at this table. [*She lights a lamp on the table.*] No ink! [*She takes the inkstand to the cupboard and fills it from an ink-bottle.*] How sad it is to see them go!
[MME VOITSKAYA *comes slowly in.*]

MME VOITSKAYA: They have gone.

[*She sits down and at once becomes absorbed in her book.*]

[SONIA *sits down at the table and looks through an account book.*]

SONIA: First, Uncle Vanya, let us write up the accounts. They are in a dreadful state. Come, begin. You take one and I will take the other.

VOITSKI: In account with — [*They sit silently writing.*]

MARINA [*yawning*]: The sand-man has come.

ASTROFF: How still it is. Their pens scratch, the cricket sings; it is so warm and comfortable. I hate to go.

[*The tinkling of bells is heard.*]

ASTROFF: My carriage has come. There now remains but to say good-bye to you, my friends, and to my table here, and then — away! [*He puts the map into the portfolio.*]

MARINA: Don't hurry away; sit a little longer with us.

ASTROFF: Impossible.

VOITSKI [*writing*]: And carry forward from the old debt two seventy-five —

[WORKMAN *comes in.*]

WORKMAN: Your carriage is waiting, sir.

ASTROFF: All right. [*He hands the* WORKMAN *his medicine-case, portfolio, and box.*] Look out, don't crush the portfolio!

WORKMAN: Very well, sir. [*Exit.*]

SONIA: When shall we see you again?

ASTROFF: Hardly before next summer. Probably not this winter, though, of course if anything should happen you will let me know. [*He shakes hands with them.*] Thank you for your kindness, for your hospitality, for everything!

[*He goes up to* MARINA *and kisses her head.*] Good-bye old nurse!

MARINA: Are you going without your tea?

ASTROFF: I don't want any, nurse.

MARINA: Won't you have a drop of vodka?

ASTROFF [*hesitatingly*]: Yes, I might.

[MARINA *goes out.*]

ASTROFF [*after a pause*]: My off-wheeler has gone lame for some reason. I noticed it yesterday when Peter was taking him to water.

VOITSKI: You should have him re-shod.

ASTROFF: I shall have to go around by the blacksmith's on my way home. It can't be avoided. [*He stands looking up at the map of Africa hanging on the wall.*] I suppose it is roasting hot in Africa now.

VOITSKI: Yes, I suppose it is.

[MARINA *comes back carrying a tray on which are a glass of vodka and a piece of bread.*]

MARINA: Help yourself. [ASTROFF *drinks.*] To your good health; [*She bows deeply.*] Eat your bread with it.

ASTROFF: No, I like it so. And now, good-bye. [*To* MARINA.] You needn't come out to see me off, nurse.

[*He goes out.* SONIA *follows him with a candle to light him to the carriage.* MARINA *sits down in her armchair.*]

VOITSKI [*writing*]: On the 2nd of February, twenty pounds of butter; on the 16th, twenty pounds of butter again. Buck-wheat flour — [*A pause. Bells are heard tinkling.*]

MARINA: He has gone. [*A pause.*]

[SONIA *comes in and sets the candlestick on the table.*]

SONIA: He has gone.

VOITSKI [*adding and writing*]: Total, fifteen — twenty-five —

[SONIA *sits down and begins to write.*]

MARINA [*yawning*]: Oh, ho! The Lord have mercy.

[TELEGIN *comes in on tiptoe, sits down near the door, and begins to tune his guitar.*]

VOITSKI [*to* SONIA, *stroking her hair*]: Oh, my child, I am so miserable; if you only knew how miserable I am!

SONIA: What can we do? We must live our lives. [*A pause.*] Yes, we shall live, Uncle Vanya. We shall live through the long procession of days before us, and through the long evenings; we shall patiently bear the trials that fate imposes on us; we shall work for others without rest, both now and when we are old; and when our last hour comes we shall meet it humbly, and there, beyond the grave, we shall say that we have suffered and wept, that our life was bitter, and God will have pity on us. Ah, then, dear Uncle, we shall see that bright and beautiful life; we shall rejoice and look back upon our sorrow here; a tender smile —

and — we shall rest. I have faith, Uncle, fervent, passionate faith. [SONIA *kneels down before her uncle and lays her head on his hands. She speaks in a weary voice.*] We shall rest. [TELEGIN *plays softly on the guitar.*] We shall rest. We shall hear the angels. We shall see heaven shining like a jewel. We shall see all evil and all our pain sink away in the great compassion that shall enfold the world. Our life will be as peaceful and tender and sweet as a caress. I have faith; I have faith. [*She wipes away her tears.*] My poor, poor Uncle Vanya, you are crying! [*Weeping.*] You have never known what happiness was, but wait, Uncle Vanya, wait! We shall rest. [*She embraces him.*]

We shall rest. [*The* WATCHMAN'S *rattle is heard in the garden;* TELEGIN *plays softly;* MME VOITSKAYA *writes something on the margin of her pamphlet;* MARINA *knits her stocking.*] We shall rest.

QUESTIONS AND DISCUSSION POINTS

1. How can the inclusion of prosaic details of farm accounts be artistically justified?

2. How does Chekhov indicate his attitude to the characters involved in this scene?

3. Do the characters' personalities emerge from the way they speak?

4. What saves Sonia's final speech from being merely passive acquiescence in the prospect of endless drudgery?

5. How would you tackle a reply to the protest, 'But nothing really happens in this scene'?

6. How would you describe the 'atmosphere' of this episode? How does Chekhov create it?

THE IRISH CONTRIBUTION

GEORGE BERNARD SHAW

Saint Joan

Saint Joan (1923) is the play which established Shaw in popular estimation as the greatest living English dramatist. His plays had been commercially successful for some twenty years but *Saint Joan* was immediately recognized as his finest achievement. As an avowed disciple of Ibsen, Shaw had been a controversial figure for many years, often antagonizing particular groups through plays such as *Major Barbara* or *The Doctor's Dilemma*.

In *Saint Joan*, the historical framework and Shaw's shrewd recognition of the dramatic impact of the transcripts of the original trial prevented the didacticism and opinion-mongering which had blighted many of his previous plays from being over-prominent. He himself seemed to recognize this, for he is reported to have said to Sybil Thorndike, who played Joan in the London production of March, 1924: 'It is the easiest play I have ever had to write. All I've done is to put down the facts, to arrange Joan for the stage.'

The play tells the story of the French exploitation, in their war against the English forces, of Joan's inspiring leadership, and their subsequent rejection of her as a supposed heretic. Joan is shown in the early scenes as a vigorously determined country girl with a strong sense of her divine mission, who through her enthusiasm gradually gains the confidence of the French rulers and people. She plays a large part in the French counter-offensive against the English but once Charles has been crowned at Rheims, there is a noticeable cooling-off on the part of the French, who are now anxious to make a treaty with the English. Joan's luck, or inspiration, finally deserts her and she is captured by the English, who hand her over to the court of the Inquisition as a heretic. Shaw shows clearly that the political forces of England, as represented by Warwick, and the religious forces of France, as represented by Cauchon, see her as a real threat to their supremacy and are anxious to be rid of her, though hiding their real motives under talk of heresy.

In the concluding scene of the play, Joan is gradually defeated by the machinations of Cauchon, Warwick and the Inquisition, in spite of the sincere efforts to convert her of some members of the court, and is burnt as a heretic. In a piercingly ironical Epilogue, Shaw asserts that Joan would be treated in exactly the same way in the Twentieth Century as in the Fifteenth by those who in any age resent a challenge to their entrenched beliefs.

*   *   *   *   *

The following episode, from Scene Six, shows Joan's final realization of her helplessness before the sophistry, cunning and ruthlessness of her opponents, and her final resolution to die rather than live in captivity. Here she achieves a truly tragic awareness of her own nature and of that of the world which has rejected her, and which she now rejects. There is here none of the tedious Shavian preaching or theorizing, and as a result his writing takes on a directness and passion which show his great dramatic gifts.

Extract from *Saint Joan*

Pp. 135–140 of Penguin edition.

LADVENU [*rising with the paper in his hand*]: My Lord: here is the form of recantation for The Maid to sign.

CAUCHON: Read it to her.

JOAN: Do not trouble. I will sign it.

THE INQUISITOR: Woman: you must know what you are putting your hand to. Read it to her, Brother Martin. And let all be silent.

LADVENU [*reading quietly*]: 'I, Joan, commonly called The Maid, a miserable sinner, do confess that I have most grievously sinned in the following articles. I have pretended to have revelations from God and the angels and the blessed saints, and perversely rejected the Church's warnings that these were temptations by demons. I have blasphemed abominably by wearing an immodest dress, contrary to the Holy Scripture and the canons of the Church. Also I have clipped my hair in the style of a man, and, against all the duties which have made my sex specially acceptable in heaven, have taken up the sword, even to the shedding of human blood, inciting men to slay each other, invoking evil spirits to delude them, and stubbornly and most blasphemously imputing these sins to Almighty God. I confess to the sin of sedition, to the sin of idolatry, to the sin of disobedience, to the sin of pride, and to the sin of heresy. All of which sins I now renounce and abjure and depart from, humbly thanking you Doctors and Masters who have brought me back to the truth and into the grace of our Lord. And I will never return to my errors, but will remain in communion with our Holy Church and in obedience to our Holy Father the Pope of Rome. All this I swear by God Almighty and the Holy Gospels, in witness whereto I sign my name to this recantation.'

THE INQUISITOR: You understand this, Joan?

JOAN [*listless*]: It is plain enough, sir.

THE INQUISITOR: And is it true?

51

JOAN: It may be true. If it were not true, the fire would not be ready for me in the market-place.

LADVENU [*taking up his pen and a book, and coming to her quickly lest she should compromise herself again*]: Come, child: let me guide your hand. Take the pen. [*She does so; and they begin to write, using the book as a desk.*]

J.E.H.A.N.E. So. Now make your mark by yourself.

JOAN [*makes her mark, and gives him back the pen, tormented by the rebellion of her soul against her mind and body*]: There!

LADVENU [*replacing the pen on the table, and handing the recantation to* CAUCHON *with a reverence*]: Praise be to God, my brothers, the lamb has returned to the flock; and the shepherd rejoices in her more than in ninety and nine just persons. [*He returns to his seat.*]

THE INQUISITOR [*taking the paper from* CAUCHON]: We declare thee by this act set free from the danger of excommunication in which thou stoodest. [*He throws the paper down to the table.*]

JOAN: I thank you.

THE INQUISITOR: But because thou has sinned most presumptuously against God and the Holy Church, and that thou mayest repent thy errors in solitary contemplation, and be shielded from all temptation to return to them, we, for the good of thy soul, and for a penance that may wipe out thy sins and bring thee finally unspotted to the throne of grace, do condemn thee to eat the bread of sorrow and drink the water of affliction to the end of thy earthly days in perpetual imprisonment.

JOAN [*rising in consternation and terrible anger*]: Perpetual imprisonment! Am I not then to be set free?

LADVENU [*mildly shocked*]: Set free, child, after such wickedness as yours! What are you dreaming of?

JOAN: Give me that writing. [*She rushes to the table; snatches up the paper; and tears it into fragments*]: Light your fire: do you think I dread it as much as the life of a rat in a hole? My voices were right.

LADVENU: Joan! Joan!

JOAN: Yes: they told me you were fools [*the word gives great offence*], and that I was not to listen to your fine words nor trust to your charity. You promised me my life; but you lied [*indignant exclamations*]. You think that life is nothing but not being stone dead. It is not the bread and water I fear: I can live on bread: when have I asked for more? It is no hardship to drink water if the water be clean. Bread has no sorrow for me, and water no affliction. But to shut me from the light of the sky and the sight of the fields and flowers; to chain my feet so that I can never again ride with the soldiers nor climb the hills; to make me breathe foul damp darkness, and keep me from everything that brings me back to the love of God when your wickedness and foolishness tempt me to hate Him: all this is worse than the furnace in the Bible that was heated seven times. I could do without my warhorse; I could drag about in a skirt; I could let the banners and the trumpets and the knights and soldiers pass me and leave me behind as they leave the other women, if only I could still hear the wind in the trees, the larks in the sunshine, the young lambs crying through the healthy frost, and the blessed blessed church bells that send my angel voices floating to me on the wind. But without these things I cannot live; and by your wanting to take them away from me, or from any human creature, I know that your counsel is of the devil, and that mine is of God.

THE ASSESSORS [*in great commotion*]: Blasphemy! blasphemy! She is possessed. She said our counsel was of the devil. And hers of God. Monstrous! The devil is in our midst, etc., etc.

D'ESTIVET [*shouting above the din*]: She is a relapsed heretic, obstinate, incorrigible, and altogether unworthy of the mercy we have shewn her. I call for her excommunication.

THE CHAPLAIN [*to* THE EXECUTIONER]: Light your fire, man. To the stake with her.

[THE EXECUTIONER *and his assistants hurry out through the courtyard.*]

LADVENU: You wicked girl: if your counsel were of God would He not deliver you?

JOAN: His ways are not your ways. He wills that I go through the fire to His bosom; for I am His child, and you are not fit that I should live among you. That is my last word to you.

[*The soldiers seize her.*]

CAUCHON [*rising*]: Not yet.

[*They wait. There is a dead silence.* CAUCHON *turns to* THE INQUISITOR *with an inquiring look.* THE INQUISITOR *nods affirmatively. They rise solemnly, and intone the sentence antiphonally.*]

CAUCHON: We decree that thou art a relapsed heretic.

THE INQUISITOR: Cast out from the unity of the Church.

CAUCHON: Sundered from her body.

THE INQUISITOR: Infected with the leprosy of heresy.

CAUCHON: A member of Satan.

THE INQUISITOR: We declare that thou must be excommunicate.

CAUCHON: And now we do cast thee out, segregate thee, and abandon thee to the secular power.

THE INQUISITOR: Admonishing the same secular power that it moderate its judgment of thee in respect of death and division of the limbs. [*He resumes his seat.*]

CAUCHON: And if any true sign of penitence appear in thee, to permit our Brother Martin to administer to thee the sacrament of penance.

THE CHAPLAIN: Into the fire with the witch [*he rushes at her, and helps the soldiers to push her out*].

[JOAN *is taken away through the courtyard. The assessors rise in disorder, and follow the soldiers, except* LADVENU, *who has hidden his face in his hands.*]

CAUCHON [*rising again in the act of sitting down*]: No, no: this is irregular. The representative of the secular arm should be here to receive her from us.

THE INQUISITOR [*also on his feet again*]: That man is an incorrigible fool.

CAUCHON: Brother Martin: see that everything is done in order.

LADVENU: My place is at her side, my Lord. You must exercise your own authority. [*He hurries out.*]

CAUCHON: These English are impossible: they will thrust her straight into the fire. Look!

[*He points to the courtyard, in which the glow and flicker of fire can now be seen reddening the May daylight. Only the* BISHOP *and the* INQUISITOR *are left in the court.*]

CAUCHON [*turning to go*]: We must stop that.

THE INQUISITOR [*calmly*]: Yes; but not too fast, my lord.

CAUCHON [*halting*]: But there is not a moment to lose.

THE INQUISITOR: We have proceeded in perfect order. If the English choose to put themselves in the wrong, it is not our business to put them in the right. A flaw in the procedure may be useful later on: one never knows. And the sooner it is over, the better for that poor girl.

CAUCHON [*relaxing*]: That is true. But I suppose we must see this dreadful thing through.

THE INQUISITOR: One gets used to it. Habit is everything. I am accustomed to the fire: it is soon over. But it is a terrible thing to see a young and innocent creature crushed between these mighty forces, the Church and the Law.

CAUCHON: You call her innocent!

THE INQUISITOR: Oh, quite innocent. What does she know of the Church and the Law? She did not understand a word we were saying. It is the ignorant who suffer. Come, or we shall be late for the end.

CAUCHON [*going with him*]: I shall not be sorry if we are: I am not so accustomed as you.

[*They are going out when* WARWICK *comes in, meeting them.*]

WARWICK. Oh, I am intruding. I thought it was all over.

[*He makes a feint of retiring.*]

CAUCHON: Do not go, my lord. It is all over.

THE INQUISITOR: The execution is not in our hands, my lord; but it is desirable that we should witness the end. So by your leave — [*He bows, and goes out through the courtyard.*]

CAUCHON: There is some doubt whether your people have observed the forms of law, my lord.

WARWICK: I am told that there is some doubt whether your

C

authority runs in this city, my lord. It is not in your diocese. However, if you will answer for that I will answer for the rest.

CAUCHON: It is to God that we both must answer. Good morning, my lord.

WARWICK: My lord: good morning.

[*They look at one another for a moment with unconcealed hostility.*]

QUESTIONS AND DISCUSSION POINTS

1. Does the length of Joan's main speeches detract from the dramatic force of the episode? If not, why not?

2. How does Shaw convey his attitude to subsidiary characters? Which of them is most sympathetically portrayed?

3. Which would you say is the most dramatically effective moment in this episode?

4. 'A young and innocent creature crushed between these mighty forces, the Church and the Law.' Do you think this summary does justice to the situation shown in this episode?

5. How prominent a part does irony play in the style of this episode?

6. Have you any comment on Shaw's use of stage directions and interpretative remarks?

JOHN MILLINGTON SYNGE

The Playboy of the Western World

THE first productions of *The Playboy of the Western World* (1907) provoked from the Abbey Theatre audiences a fiercely, and sometimes hysterically, critical response. The objections were to what the audiences saw as the shamelessness, cruelty and blasphemy of the play. The fundamental criticism of Ireland which the play makes, as a country blind to everything but its own absurdly idealized image seems to have escaped the notice of these early audiences. The myth of a 'heroic' Ireland had been widely celebrated in the Nineties, by the young Yeats among others. Like the mature Yeats, Synge saw the Irish weakness for self-dramatization and idealization as an obstruction to the development of the Irish nation and character. Synge's wider views on these issues were ignored, however, in the absurd furore over trivialities. Lady Gregory recalled, for example, that the first two acts of the play were quite well received by the first night audience and that only the mention of the word 'shift' near the end of the play caused the audience to express its disapproval by hissing or walking out. It seems that a large part of the audience construed the mention of this garment as a slight on the purity of Irish womanhood!

Such reactions now seem supremely irrelevant. At a distance of almost sixty years, the play can be seen for what it is, a masterpiece of searching, controlled irony, a carefully constructed revelation of what Synge saw as the Irish nation's tragic flaw. Synge's irony is conveyed through the medium of his mastery of spoken Irish dialect and his delight in the vividness of imagery and variety of rhythm which characterize this speech.

The scene of most of the play is a country public house in County Mayo, kept by Michael James Flaherty and his daughter, Pegeen Mike. The hard-drinking life of the rather garrulous Michael James and his neighbours is portrayed in the opening scenes but their routine life is disrupted by the arrival of Christy Mahon who, with a tale of how he killed his father so as to throw off the parental yoke, wins the heart of Pegeen Mike in spite of her former plans to marry one of her neighbours, Shawn Keogh. Christy's self-esteem is increased by the further designs on him of the Widow Quin. In an atmosphere of adulation and awe, Christy's personality becomes more extravert, more positive, and his performance in the local horse races clinches his popularity and self-confidence.

This new-found self-confidence is severely tested by the re-appearance of his father, whom he had only stunned in his attack, for his father, domineering as ever, tries to cow him once more. Christy, however, having tasted popularity and power, resists his father's bullying to the point of killing him, as he thinks. The deed which he had narrated and which had been largely responsible for his popularity now happens before the eyes of his future wife and her friends, but the actuality terrifies where the story had delighted, and Christy is rejected by those who had formerly lionized him, including Pegeen Mike. Christy is brutally captured and con-demned by these former friends.

Once again, however, Christy's father survives the apparently fatal attack and his re-appearance sets Christy free. Christy's experiences have not been wasted on him, however, for he now establishes a moral superiority over his father and leaves behind the hypocrites who had betrayed him. Pegeen, left among the medio-crities and hypocrites, bewails his departure, finally realizing the implications of her betrayal of her 'playboy', Christy, and of herself. She has been faced by the challenge of love and possible suffering and the challenge has proved too much for her.

The play, then, is a celebration of one man's struggle to free himself from convention, to break down the barrier between idyll and reality, and an analysis and satire of the conventions and deceptions in which the weak are still enmeshed.

*   *   *   *   *

The following extract is the conclusion of the play. Here Christy finally asserts his individuality and Pegeen is faced with the choice between the playboy and the dull predictability of her former life as represented by Shawn, Michael, Philly and the rest.

Extract from *The Playboy of the Western World*

Pp. 224–229 of T. R. Henn edition (Methuen)

MAHON [*making a grab at* CHRISTY]: Come here to me.

CHRISTY [*more threateningly*]: Leave me go, I'm saying.

MAHON: I will, maybe, when your legs is limping, and your back is blue.

CROWD: Keep it up, the two of you. I'll back the old one. Now the playboy.

CHRISTY [*in low and intense voice*]: Shut your yelling, for if you're after making a mighty man of me this day by the power of a lie, you're setting me now to think if it's a poor thing to be lonesome it's worse, maybe, to go mixing with the fools of earth.

[MAHON *makes a movement towards him.*]

[*Almost shouting.*] Keep off . . . lest I do show a blow unto the lot of you would set the guardian angels winking in the clouds above. [*He swings round with a sudden rapid movement and picks up a loy.*]

CROWD [*half frightened, half amused*]: He's going mad! Mind yourselves! Run from the idiot!

CHRISTY: If I am an idiot, I'm after hearing my voice this day would raise the top-knot on a poet in a merchant's town. I've won your racing, and your lepping, and . . .

MAHON: Shut your gullet and come on with me.

CHRISTY: I'm going, but I'll stretch you first.

[*He runs at old* MAHON *with the loy, chases him out of the door, followed by crowd and* WIDOW QUIN. *There is a great noise outside, then a yell, and dead silence for a moment.* CHRISTY *comes in, half dazed, and goes to fire.*]

WIDOW QUIN [*coming in hurriedly, and going to him*]: They're turning again you. Come on, or you'll be hanged, indeed.

CHRISTY: I'm thinking, from this out, Pegeen'll be giving me praises, the same as in the hours gone by.

WIDOW QUIN [*impatiently*]: Come by the back door. I'd think bad to have you stifled on the gallows tree.

CHRISTY [*indignantly*]: I will not, then. What good'd be my lifetime if I left Pegeen?

WIDOW QUIN: Come on, and you'll be no worse than you were
last night; and you with a double murder this time to be telling
to the girls.

CHRISTY: I'll not leave Pegeen Mike.

WIDOW QUIN [*impatiently*]: Isn't there the match of her in every
parish public, from Binghamstown unto the plain of Meath?
Come on, I tell you, and I'll find you finer sweethearts at each
waning moon.

CHRISTY: It's Pegeen I'm seeking only, and what'd I care if you
brought me a drift of chosen females, standing in their shifts
itself, maybe, from this place to the eastern world?

SARA [*runs in, pulling off one of her petticoats*]: They're going to hang
him. [*Holding out petticoat and shawl.*]
Fit these upon him, and let him run off to the east.

WIDOW QUIN: He's raving now; but we'll fit them on him, and
I'll take him in the ferry to the Achill boat.

CHRISTY [*struggling feebly*]: Leave me go, will you? when I'm
thinking of my luck today, for she will wed me surely, and I a
proven hero in the end of all.
[*They try to fasten petticoat round him.*]

WIDOW QUIN: Take his left hand and we'll pull him now. Come
on, young fellow.

CHRISTY [*suddenly starting up*]: You'll be taking me from her?
You're jealous, is it, of her wedding me? Go on from this.
[*He snatches up a stool, and threatens them with it.*]

WIDOW QUIN [*going*]: It's in the madhouse they should put him,
not in jail, at all. We'll go by the back door to call the doctor, and
we'll save him so.
[*She goes out, with* SARA, *through inner room. Men crowd in the
doorway.* CHRISTY *sits down again by the fire.*]

MICHAEL [*in a terrified whisper*]: Is the old lad killed surely?

PHILLY: I'm after feeling the last gasps quitting his heart.
[*They peer in at* CHRISTY.]

MICHAEL [*with a rope*]: Look at the way he is. Twist a hangman's knot on it, and slip it over his head, while he's not minding at all.

PHILLY: Let you take it, Shaneen. You're the soberest of all that's here.

SHAWN: Is it me to go near him, and he the wickedest and worst with me? Let you take it, Pegeen Mike.

PEGEEN: Come on, so.

[*She goes forward with the others, and they drop the double hitch over his head.*]

CHRISTY: What ails you?

SHAWN [*triumphantly, as they pull the rope tight on his arms*]: Come on to the peelers, till they stretch you now.

CHRISTY: Me!

MICHAEL: If we took pity on you the Lord God would, maybe, bring us ruin from the law today, so you'd best come easy, for hanging is an easy and a speedy end.

CHRISTY: I'll not stir. [*To* PEGEEN]. And what is it you'll say to me, and I after doing it this time in the face of all?

PEGEEN: I'll say, a strange man is a marvel, with his mighty talk; but what's a squabble in your back yard, and the blow of a loy, have taught me that there's a great gap between a gallous story and a dirty deed. [*To men.*] Take him on from this, or the lot of us will be likely put on trial for his deed today.

CHRISTY [*with horror in his voice*]: And its yourself will send me off, to have a horny-fingered hangman hitching slipknots at the butt of my ear.

MEN [*pulling rope*]: Come on, will you?

[*He is pulled down to the floor.*]

CHRISTY [*twisting his legs round the table*]: Cut the rope, Pegeen, and I'll quit the lot of you, and live from this out, like the madman of Keel, eating muck and green weeds on the faces of the cliffs.

PEGEEN: And leave us to hang, is it, for a saucy liar, the like of you? [*To* MEN]. Take him on, out from this.

SHAWN: Pull a twist on his neck, and squeeze him so.

PHILLY: Twist yourself. Sure he cannot hurt you, if you keep your distance from his teeth alone.

SHAWN: I'm afeared of him. [*To* PEGEEN.] Lift a lighted sod, will you, and scotch his leg.

PEGEEN [*blowing the fire with a bellows*]: Leave go now, young fellow, or I'll scorch your shins.

CHRISTY: You're blowing for to torture me. [*His voice rising and growing stronger.*] That's your kind, is it? Then let the lot of you be wary, for, if I've to face the gallows, I'll have a gay march down, I tell you, and shed the blood of some of you before I die.

SHAWN [*in terror*]: Keep a good hold, Philly. Be wary, for the love of God. For I'm thinking he would liefest wreak his pains on me.

CHRISTY [*almost gaily*]: If I do lay my hands on you, it's the way you'll be at the fall of night, hanging as a scarecrow for the fowls of hell. Ah, you'll have a gallous jaunt, I'm saying, coaching out through limbo with my father's ghost.

SHAWN [*to* PEGEEN]: Make haste, will you? Oh, isn't he a holy terror, and isn't it true for Father Reilly, that all drink's a curse that has the lot of you so shaky and uncertain now?

CHRISTY: If I can wring a neck among you, I'll have a royal judgment looking on the trembling jury in the courts of law. And won't there be crying out in May the day I'm stretched upon the rope, with ladies in their silks and satins snivelling in their lacy kerchiefs, and they rhyming songs and ballads on the terror of my fate? [*He squirms round on the floor and bites* SHAWN'S *leg.*]

SHAWN [*shrieking*]: My leg's bit on me. He's the like of a mad dog, I'm thinking, the way that I will surely die.

CHRISTY [*delighted with himself*]: You will, then, the way you can shake out hell's flags of welcome for my coming in two weeks or three, for I'm thinking Satan hasn't many have killed their da in Kerry, and in Mayo too.

[*Old* MAHON *comes in behind on all fours and looks on unnoticed.*]

MEN [*to* PEGEEN]: Bring the sod, will you?

PEGEEN [*coming over*]: God help him so. [*Burns his leg.*]

CHRISTY [*kicking and screaming*]: Oh, glory be to God!

[*He kicks loose from the table, and they all drag him towards the door.*]

JIMMY [*seeing old* MAHON]: Will you look what's come in?
[*They all drop* CHRISTY *and run left.*]

CHRISTY [*scrambling on his knees face to face with old* MAHON]:
Are you coming to be killed a third time, or what ails you
now?

MAHON: For what is it they have you tied?

CHRISTY: They're taking me to the peelers to have me hanged for
slaying you.

MICHAEL [*apologetically*]: It is the will of God that all should guard
their little cabins from the treachery of law, and what would my
daughter be doing if I was ruined or was hanged itself?

MAHON [*grimly, loosening* CHRISTY]: It's little I care if you put a
bag on her back, and went picking cockles till the hour of death;
but my son and myself will be going our own way, and we'll
have great times from this out telling stories of the villainy of
Mayo, and the fools is here. [*To* CHRISTY, *who is freed.*] Come on
now.

CHRISTY: Go with you, is it? I will then, like a gallant captain with
his heathen slave. Go on now and I'll see you from this day
stewing my oatmeal and washing my spuds, for I'm master of all
fights from now. [*Pushing* MAHON.] Go on, I'm saying.

MAHON: Is it me?

CHRISTY: Not a word out of you. Go on from this.

MAHON: [*walking out and looking back at* CHRISTY *over his shoulder*]:
Glory be to God! [*With a broad smile.*] I am crazy again.
[*Goes.*]

CHRISTY: Ten thousand blessings upon all that's here, for you've
turned me a likely gaffer in the end of all, the way I'll go romanc-
ing through a romping lifetime from this hour to the dawning of
the Judgment Day.
[*He goes out.*]

MICHAEL: By the will of God, we'll have peace now for our drinks.
Will you draw the porter, Pegeen?

SHAWN [*going up to her*]: It's a miracle Father Reilly can wed us in
the end of all, and we'll have none to trouble us when his vicious
bite is healed.

PEGEEN [*hitting him a box on the ear*]: Quit my sight.
[*Putting her shawl over her head and breaking out into wild lamenta-
tions.*] Oh, my grief, I've lost him surely. I've lost the only
Playboy of the Western World.

CURTAIN

QUESTIONS AND DISCUSSION POINTS

1. Define as exactly as you can the object of Synge's satire in this
   episode, and say whether you think it successful.

2. Illustrate Synge's command of spoken Irish.

3. What lessons have enabled Christy to become 'a likely gaffer in
   the end of all'?

4. What do you think is the point of Mahon's parting remark:
   'I am crazy again'?

5. Are the comic, satirical and tragic elements successfully recon-
   ciled?

6. Pegeen's remark, 'there's a great gap between a gallous story
   and a dirty deed,' has been called the heart of the play. Discuss
   the meaning of this comment.

SEAN O'CASEY

Juno and the Paycock

Juno and the Paycock (1924) was enthusiastically received by the audience of the Abbey Theatre, where it was first produced, and consolidated O'Casey's growing reputation, a reputation, incidentally, which was subsequently shattered by *The Plough and the Stars* (1926), which provoked riots on the second night of its run at the Abbey Theatre. In his *Autobiographies*, O'Casey remarks with a sly irony that after the production of *Juno and the Paycock*: 'Yeats halted in his meditations to tell Sean that he had given new hope and new life to the theatre.' After the reception of *The Plough and the Stars*, O'Casey left Ireland for England, sickened by the world of the Abbey Theatre and Dublin's literary cliques, by 'their sneering lofty conception of what they called culture.' Loyal to the work of Ibsen, Strindberg and Shaw, O'Casey was increasingly repelled by the fickleness and superficial modishness of the Irish critics, some of whom were, by 1926, beginning to apply to his work such labels as 'the drama of the dregs.' He was above all an outspoken individualist and felt himself limited by this milieu: 'Some had said he was another Chekhov, others, a Dickens, and another Ben Jonson. He knew himself that he was like Sean O'Casey, and he was determined to be like no-one else; for better or worse, for richer or poorer, so help him God!'

Like all Irishmen of his generation, O'Casey was profoundly affected by Ireland's struggles for independence, admiring the courage of Irishmen yet appalled by their simplicity and the tragic waste involved in the fighting. In *Juno*, Captain Jack Boyle and his drinking companion, Joxer Daly, embody O'Casey's criticism of the Irish propensity for evasion and blustering rhetoric. In the play, Boyle is directly responsible for the final unhappiness of his wife, Juno, and his daughter, Mary, and partly responsible for the death of his son, Johnny. On being told by the Englishman, Charles Bentham, that he has inherited approximately £2,000, Boyle does not bother to check the details, but plunges into an orgy of spending, and leaves his daughter to be exploited and later rejected by the plausible Bentham. Bentham is the first to discover that there has been a legal mistake which means that Boyle will inherit virtually nothing, and he promptly leaves the now pregnant Mary. Mary is rejected, too, by her former sweetheart, Jerry Devine, whose noble sentiments rapidly dissipate on his discovering that she is pregnant. As always, Boyle and Daly do nothing apart from indulging in sententious reflections. The background to the play is the guerilla fighting between political factions in Dublin which, characteristically, Boyle chooses to ignore: 'We've nothing to do with these things, one way or t'other. That's the Government's business an' let them do what we're paying them for doin'.' Even when his son is killed by the Republicans on the suspicion of treachery, Boyle remains what he has always been. Yet in spite of these radical criticisms of Boyle, he emerges as a wonderfully vivid and energetic character. O'Casey is not the kind of playwright moralist who can allow the characters he criticizes no degree of life.

The play is a wonderfully fine example of O'Casey's complex attitude to Ireland ('Spireland' as he sometimes called it) and its people. Compassion and criticism merge to show the poignancy of the tragedy of a naïve, evasive, but life-loving, people.

★   ★   ★   ★   ★

This episode is the end of the play, showing the final tragic consequences of Boyle's attitude towards life, as they are embodied in Mary, Johnny and Juno.

Extract from *Juno and the Paycock*

(Macmillan, St. Martin's Library, pp. 65–73)

MARY: What's up, mother? I met men carryin' away the table an' everybody's talking about us not gettin' the money after all.

MRS BOYLE: Everythin's gone wrong, Mary, everythin'. We're not gettin' a penny out o' the will, not a penny — I'll tell you all when I come back; I'm goin' for your father.

[*She runs out.*]

JOHNNY [*to* MARY, *who has sat down by the fire*]: It's a wondher you're not ashamed to show your face here, afther what has happened.

[JERRY *enters slowly; there is a look of earnest hope on his face. He looks at* MARY *for a few moments.*]

JERRY [*softly*]: Mary!

[MARY *does not answer.*]

Mary, I want to speak to you for a few moments, may I?

[MARY *remains silent;* JOHNNY *goes slowly into room on left.*]

JERRY: Your mother has told me everything, Mary, and I have come to you . . . I have come to tell you, Mary, that my love for you is greater and deeper than ever . . . .

MARY [*with a sob*]: Oh, Jerry, Jerry, say no more; all that is over now; anything like that is impossible now!

JERRY: Impossible? Why do you talk like that, Mary?

MARY: After all that has happened.

JERRY: What does it matter what has happened? We are young enough to be able to forget all those things. [*He catches her hand.*] Mary, Mary, I am pleading for your love. With Labour, Mary, humanity is above everything; we are the Leaders in the fight for a new life. I want to forget Bentham, I want to forget that you left me — even for a while.

MARY: Oh, Jerry, Jerry, you haven't the bitter word of scorn for me after all.

JERRY [*passionately*]: Scorn! I love you, love you, Mary!

MARY [*rising, and looking him in the eyes*]: Even though . . .

JERRY: Even though you threw me over for another man; even though you gave me many a bitter word!

MARY: Yes, yes, I know; but you love me, even though . . . even though . . . I'm . . . goin' . . . goin' . . . [*He looks at her questioningly and fear gathers in his eyes.*] Ah, I was thinkin' so . . . You don't know everything!

JERRY [*poignantly*]: Surely to God, Mary, you don't mean that . . . that . . . that . . . .

MARY: Now you know all, Jerry; now you know all!

JERRY: My God, Mary, have you fallen as low as that?

MARY: Yes, Jerry, as you say, I have fallen as low as that.

JERRY: I didn't mean it that way, Mary . . . it came on me so sudden, that I didn't mind what I was sayin' . . . I never expected this — your mother never told me . . . I'm sorry . . . God knows, I'm sorry for you, Mary.

MARY: Let us say no more, Jerry; I don't blame you for thinkin' it's terrible . . . I suppose it is . . . Everybody'll think the same . . . it's only as I expected — your humanity is just as narrow as the humanity of the others.

JERRY: I'm sorry, all the same . . . I shouldn't have troubled you . . . I wouldn't if I'd known . . . If I can do anything for you . . . Mary . . . I will.

[*He turns to go, and halts at the door.*]

MARY: Do you remember, Jerry, the verses you read when you gave the lecture in the Socialist Rooms some time ago, on Humanity's Strife with Nature?

JERRY: The verses — no; I don't remember them.

MARY: I do. They're runnin' in me head now —

> An' we felt the power that fashion'd
> All the lovely things we saw,
> That created all the murmur
> Of an everlasting law,
> Was a hand of force an' beauty,
> With an eagle's tearin' claw.

Then we saw our globe of beauty
Was an ugly thing as well,
A hymn divine whose chorus
Was an agonizin' yell;
Like the story of a demon,
That an angel had to tell;

Like a glowin' picture by a
Hand unsteady, brought to ruin;
Life her craters, if their deadness
Could give life unto the moon;
Like the agonizing horror
Of a violin out of tune.

[*There is a pause, and* DEVINE *goes slowly out.*]

JOHNNY [*returning*]: Is he gone?

MARY: Yes.

[*The two men re-enter.*]

FIRST MAN: We can't wait any longer for t'oul' fella — sorry, Miss, but we have to live as well as th'nex' man.

[*They carry out some things.*]

JOHNNY: Oh, isn't this terrible! . . . I suppose you told him everything . . . couldn't you have waited for a few days? . . . he'd have stopped th'takin' of the things, if you'd kep' your mouth shut. Are you burnin' to tell every one of the shame you've brought on us?

MARY [*snatching up her cat and coat*]: Oh, this is unbearable!

[*She rushes out.*]

FIRST MAN [*re-entering*]: We'll take the chest o' drawers next — it's the heaviest.

[*The votive light flickers for a moment, and goes out.*]

JOHNNY [*in a cry of fear*]: Mother o' God, the light's afther goin' out!

FIRST MAN: You put the win' up me the way you bawled that time. That oil's all gone, that's all.

JOHNNY [*with an agonizing cry*]: Mother o' God, there's a shot I'm afther gettin'!

FIRST MAN: What's wrong with you, man? Is it a fit you're takin'?

JOHNNY: I'm afther feelin' a pain in me breast, like the tearin' by of a bullet!

FIRST MAN: He's goin' mad — it's a wondher they'd leave a chap like that here by himself.

[*Two Irregulars enter swiftly; they carry revolvers; one goes over to* JOHNNY; *the other covers the two furniture men.*]

FIRST IRREGULAR [*to the men, quietly and incisively*]: Who are you? what are yous doin' here? — quick!

FIRST MAN: Removin' furniture that's not paid for.

IRREGULAR: Get over to the other end of the room an' turn your faces to the wall — quick!

[*The two men turn their faces to the wall, with their hands up.*]

SECOND IRREGULAR [*to* JOHNNY]: Come on, Sean Boyle, you're wanted; some of us have a word to say to you.

JOHNNY: I'm sick, I can't — what do you want with me?

SECOND IRREGULAR: Come on, come on; we've a distance to go, an' haven't much time — come on.

JOHNNY: I'm an oul' comrade — yous wouldn't shoot an oul' comrade.

SECOND IRREGULAR: Poor Tancred was an oul' comrade o' yours, but you didn't think o' that when you gave him away to the gang that sent him to his grave. But we've no time to waste: come on — here, Dermot, ketch his arm. [*To* JOHNNY.] Have you your beads?

JOHNNY: Me beads! Why do you ass me that, why do you ass me that?

SECOND IRREGULAR: Go on, go on, march!

JOHNNY: Are yous goin' to do in a comrade? — look at me arm, I lost it for Ireland.

SECOND IRREGULAR: Commandant Tancred lost his life for Ireland.

JOHNNY: Sacred Heart of Jesus, have mercy on me! Mother o' God, pray for me — be with me now in the agonies o' death! ... Hail, Mary, full o' grace ... the Lord is ... with Thee. [*They drag out* JOHNNY BOYLE, *and the curtain falls. When it rises again the most of the furniture is gone.* MARY *and* MRS BOYLE, *one on each side, are sitting in a darkened room, by the fire; it is an hour later.*]

MRS BOYLE: I'll not wait much longer . . . what did they bring him away in the mothor for? Nugent says he thinks they had guns . . . is me throubles never goin' to be over? . . . If anything ud happen to poor Johnny, I think I'd lose me mind . . . I'll go to the Police Station, surely they ought to be able to do somethin'.

[*Below is heard the sound of voices.*]

MRS BOYLE: Whisht, is that something? Maybe it's your father, though when I left him in Foley's he was hardly able to lift his head. Whisht!

[*A knock at the door, and the voice of* MRS MADIGAN, *speaking very softly*]: Mrs Boyle, Mrs Boyle. [MRS BOYLE *opens the door.*]

MRS MADIGAN: Oh, Mrs Boyle, God an' His Blessed Mother be with you this night!

MRS BOYLE [*calmly*]: What is it, Mrs Madigan? It's Johnny — something about Johnny.

MRS MADIGAN: God send it's not, God send it's not Johnny!

MRS BOYLE: Don't keep me waitin', Mrs Madigan; I've gone through so much lately that I feel able for anything.

MRS MADIGAN: Two polismen below wantin' you.

MRS BOYLE: Wantin' me; an' why do they want me?

MRS MADIGAN: Some poor fella's been found, an' they think it's, it's . . .

MRS BOYLE: Johnny, Johnny!

MARY [*with her arms round her mother*]: Oh, mother, mother, me poor, darlin' mother.

MRS BOYLE: Hush, hush, darlin'; you'll shortly have your own throuble to bear. [*To* MRS MADIGAN.] An' why do the polis think it's Johnny, Mrs Madigan?

MRS MADIGAN: Because one o' the doctors knew him when he was attendin' with his poor arm.

MRS BOYLE: Oh, it's thrue, then; it's Johnny, it's me son, me own son!

MARY: Oh, it's thrue, it's thrue what Jerry Devine says — there isn't a God, there isn't a God; if there was He wouldn't let these things happen!

MRS BOYLE: Mary, you mustn't say them things. We'll want all the help we can get from God an' His Blessed Mother now! These things have nothin' to do with the Will o' God. Ah, what can God do agen the stupidity o' men!

MRS MADIGAN: The polis want you to go with them to the hospital to see the poor body — they're waitin' below.

MRS BOYLE: We'll go. Come, Mary, an' we'll never come back here agen. Let your father furrage for himself now; I've done all I could an' it was all no use — he'll be hopeless till the end of his days. I've got a little room in me sisther's where we'll stop till your throuble is over, an' then we'll work together for the sake of the baby.

MARY: My poor little child that'll have no father!

MRS BOYLE: It'll have what's far betther — it'll have two mothers.

A ROUGH VOICE *shouting from below:* Are yous goin' to keep us waitin' for yous all night?

MRS MADIGAN [*going to the door, and shouting down*]: Take your hour, there, take your hour! If yous are in such a hurry, skip off, then, for nobody wants you here — if they did yous wouldn't be found. For you're the same as yous were undher the British Government — never where yous are wanted! As far as I can see, the Polis as Polis, in this city, is Null an' Void!

MRS BOYLE: We'll go, Mary, we'll go; you to see your poor dead brother, an' me to see me poor dead son!

MARY: I dhread it, mother, I dhread it!

MRS BOYLE: I forgot, Mary, I forgot; your poor oul' selfish mother was only thinkin' of herself. No, no, you mustn't come — it wouldn't be good for you. You go on to me sisther's an' I'll face th'ordeal meself. Maybe I didn't feel sorry enough for Mrs Tancred when her poor son was found as Johnny's been found now — because he was a Diehard! Ah, why didn't I remember that then he wasn't a Diehard or a Stater, but only a poor dead son! It's well I remember all that she said — an' it's my turn to say it now: What was the pain I suffered, Johnny, bringin' you into the world to carry you to your cradle, to the pains I'll suffer carryin' you out o' the world to bring you to your grave! Mother o' God, Mother o' God, have pity on us all! Blessed Virgin, where were you when me darlin' son was riddled with bullets, when me darlin' son was riddled with bullets? Sacred Heart o' Jesus, take away our hearts o' stone, and give us hearts o' flesh! Take away this murdherin' hate, an' give us Thine own eternal love!

[*They all go slowly out.*]

[*There is a pause; then a sound of shuffling steps on the stairs outside. The door opens and* BOYLE *and* JOXER, *both of them very drunk, enter.*]

BOYLE: I'm able to go no farther ... Two polis, ey ... what were they doin' here, I wondher? ... Up to no good, anyhow ... an' Juno an' that lovely daughter o' mine with them. [*Taking a sixpence from his pocket and looking at it.*] Wan single, solitary tanner left out of all I borreyed ... [*He lets it fall.*] The last o' the Mohicans ... The blinds is down, Joxer, the blinds is down!

JOXER [*walking unsteadily across the room, and anchoring at the bed*]: Put all ... your throubles ... in your oul' kit-bag ... an' smile ... smile ... smile!

BOYLE: The counthry'll have to steady itself ... it's goin' ... to hell ... Where'r all ... the chairs ... gone to ... steady itself, Joxer ... Chairs'll ... have to ... steady themselves ... No matther ... what any one may ... say ... Irelan's sober ... is Irelan' ... free.

JOXER [*stretching himself on the bed*]: Chains ... an' ... slaveree ... that's a darlin' motto ... a daaarlin' ... motto!

BOYLE: If th'worst comes ... to th'worse ... I can join a ... flyin' ... column ... I done ... me bit ... in Easther Week ... had no business ... to ... be ... there ... but Captain Boyle's Captain Boyle!

JOXER: Breathes there a man with soul ... so ... de ... ad ... this ... me ... o ... wn, me nat ... ive l ... an'!

BOYLE [*subsiding into a sitting posture on the floor*]: Commandant Kelly died ... in them ... arms ... Joxer ... Tell me Volunteer Butties ... says he ... that ... I died for ... Irelan'!

JOXER: D'jever rade Willie ... Reilly ... an' his own ... Colleen ... Bawn? It's a darlin' story, a daarlin' story!

BOYLE: I'm telling you ... Joxer ... th'whole worl's ... in a terr ... ible state o' ... chassis!

CURTAIN

QUESTIONS AND DISCUSSION POINTS

1. Compare O'Casey's attitude to the Irish as it is shown in this episode with Synge's.
2. What does O'Casey's use of colloquial Irish speech contribute to the total effect of this episode?
3. Which character is least, and which most, sympathetically portrayed?
4. What is the final emotion produced by this play? Pity? Anger? Impatience? Or some other?
5. What do you think is the most dramatically effective moment in this episode?
6. What do you think is the significance of Boyle's final lament, 'th'whole worl's ... in a terr ... ible state o' .... chassis!'?

THE SOCIAL DRAMATISTS

BERT BRECHT

The Good Woman of Setzuan

THIS play was written at a crucial period of Brecht's life, between 1938 and 1941, when he was living in Denmark, having fled from the Nazism which was overwhelming his native Germany. It was first performed in 1943 at Zurich Schauspielhaus. The play is typical of Brecht's 'epic theatre' in its pervasive and bitter irony, its intense didacticism and its extreme stylization. It is typically Brechtian, too, in its basic theme, the vulnerability, almost helplessness, of goodness in a fiercely and unscrupulously competitive, economically backward, society. Brecht's intention in writing the play was to show that only economic re-organization and political re-orientation could produce a society in which goodness could exist untrammelled by corrupting forces. The plight of goodness, as represented by the prostitute, Shen Te, is presented not merely to excite our sympathy and pity, but to incite us to set to rights the situation which produced the plight. The main butts of Brecht's mordant irony are the three gods, representing conventional religion, who refuse to contaminate themselves by contact with suffering humanity. Instead, they take refuge in complacent sophistry and moral admonitions. Their basic philosophy, their solution to the problem of evil, is one which Brecht angrily rejects: 'Suffering ennobles'. The play is by no means just political propaganda for Brecht's own Communist views, however. Brecht recognizes the essential and intrinsic beauty of the emotions by which man is betrayed, and this recognition gives the play its tragic poignancy and intensity. Although one might be tempted to dismiss it as a modern morality play it is much more than that.

The play concerns the search of three gods for one good person who might justify human existence: 'The resolution says: the world can go on as it is if we find enough good people, able to lead a decent human existence.' The gods have been disastrously unsuccessful in their search until, in Setzuan, they chance on Wong, a water-seller — himself a cheat — who after several failures manages to find accommodation for the gods with the prostitute, Shen Te. Hearing of her good deeds in Setzuan, the gods decide with relief that this is the person they have been searching for, and they give her money with which to establish herself in society and thus widen her sphere of influence. After buying a tobacco shop, Shen Te is ruthlessly exploited by all kinds of parasites and hangers-on, in both her business and personal affairs, so that she is forced to assume the identity of a supposed cousin, Shui Ta. The change of personality, which occurs several times in the play, is indicated by the wearing of a mask. Shui Ta fights the parasites with their own weapons and easily defeats them, establishing eventually a large tobacco factory. Meanwhile Shen Te has been exploited by Yang Sun, who coaxes her into financing his efforts to become a pilot, and promises to marry her. When she is unable to finance him fully, he rejects her. Discovering later that Shen Te was pregnant, Yang Sun accuses Shui Ta of having murdered her. Shui Ta is accordingly brought to trial, the three gods appearing as magistrates. Shen Te/Shui Ta is then forced to reveal the secret of her double identity, thus throwing into confusion the witnesses who had maligned Shen Te or Shui Ta. The gods are delighted to learn of Shen Te's survival, caution her that she must not resort to the trick of dual identity more than once a month and disappear, singing, on their clouds. They ignore Shen Te's final word in the play, 'Help!' and, their mission completed, leave only pious admonitions. The problems remain, and no permanent solution is in sight.

The plot is obviously not meant to be 'credible' in the normal sense of the word, but exists only as a vehicle for Brecht's message.

Nor is there any characterization such as provides the chief merit of many earlier plays. This play achieves its effects through the beautifully economical irony and through the pity which Brecht shows for the plight of Shen Te, though, it must be repeated, this pity is by no means an acceptance of the inevitability of the position, and never becomes sentimental.

★   ★   ★   ★   ★

The following episode is the larger part of the courtroom scene and includes the typical exhortatory Brechtian Epilogue. Brecht shows clearly that none of the witnesses are concerned with the truth, but rather with their own good.

Extract from *The Good Woman of Setzuan*

Eric Bentley translation, pp 98–110 of Penguin edition.

[*The* THIRD GOD *turns to smile at* WONG. *The* GODS *sit. The* FIRST GOD *beats on the bench with his gavel. The* POLICEMAN *brings in* SHUI TA *who walks with lordly steps. He is whistled at.*]

POLICEMAN [*to* SHUI TA]: Be prepared for a surprise. The judges have been changed.

[SHUI TA *turns quickly round, looks at them, and staggers.*]

NIECE: What's the matter now?

WIFE: The great Tobacco King nearly fainted.

HUSBAND: Yes, as soon as he saw the new judges.

WONG: Does he know who they are?

[SHUI TA *picks himself up, and the proceedings open.*]

FIRST GOD: Defendant Shui Ta, you are accused of doing away with your cousin Shen Te in order to take possession of her business. Do you plead guilty or not guilty?

SHUI TA: Not guilty, my lord.

FIRST GOD [*thumbing through the documents of the case*]: The first witness is the policeman. I shall ask him to tell us something of the respective reputations of Miss Shen Te and Mr Shui Ta.

POLICEMAN: Miss Shen Te was a young lady who aimed to please, my lord. She liked to live and let live, as the saying goes. Mr Shui Ta, on the other hand, is a man of principle. Though the generosity of Miss Shen Te forced him at times to abandon half measures, unlike the girl he was always on the side of the law, my lord. One time, he even unmasked a gang of thieves to whom his too trustful cousin had given shelter. The evidence, in short, my lord, proves that Mr Shui Ta was *incapable* of the crime of which he stands accused!

FIRST GOD: I see. And are there others who could testify along, shall we say, the same lines?

[SHU FU *rises.*]

POLICEMAN [*whispering to* GODS]: Mr Shu Fu — a very important person.

82

FIRST GOD [*inviting him to speak*]: Mr Shu Fu!

SHU FU: Mr Shui Ta is a businessman, my lord. Need I say more?

FIRST GOD: Yes.

SHU FU: Very well. I will. He is Vice President of the Council of Commerce and is about to be elected a Justice of the Peace. [*He returns to his seat.*]

[MRS MI TZU *rises.*]

WONG. Elected! He gave him the job!

[*With a gesture the* FIRST GOD *asks who* MRS MI TZU *is.*]

POLICEMAN: Another very important person. Mrs Mi Tzu.

FIRST GOD [*inviting her to speak*]: Mrs Mi Tzu!

MRS MI TZU: My lord, as Chairman of the Committee on Social Work, I wish to call attention to just a couple of eloquent facts: Mr Shui Ta not only has erected a model factory with model housing in our city, he is a regular contributor to our home for the disabled. [*She returns to her seat.*]

POLICEMAN [*whispering*]: And she's a great friend of the judge that ate the goose!

FIRST GOD [*to the* POLICEMAN]: Oh, thank you. What next? [*To the Court, genially*] Oh, yes. We should find out if any of the evidence is less favourable to the defendant.

[WONG, *the* CARPENTER, *the* OLD MAN, *the* OLD WOMAN, *the* UNEMPLOYED MAN, *the* SISTER-IN-LAW, *and the* NIECE *come forward.*]

POLICEMAN [*whispering*]: Just the riff-raff, my lord.

FIRST GOD [*addressing the 'riff-raff'*]: Well, um, riff-raff — do you know anything of the defendant, Mr Shui Ta?

WONG: Too much, my lord.

UNEMPLOYED MAN: What don't we know, my lord.

CARPENTER: He ruined us.

SISTER-IN-LAW: He's a cheat.

NIECE: Liar.

WIFE: Thief.

BOY: Blackmailer.

BROTHER: Murderer.

E

FIRST GOD: Thank you. We should now let the defendant state his point of view.

SHUI TA: I only came on the scene when Shen Te was in danger of losing what I had understood was a gift from the gods. Because I did the filthy jobs which someone had to do, they hate me. My activities were restricted to the minimum, my lord.

SISTER-IN-LAW: He had us arrested!

SHUI TA: Certainly. You stole from the bakery!

SISTER-IN-LAW: Such concern for the bakery! You didn't want the shop for yourself, I suppose!

SHUI TA: I didn't want the shop overrun with parasites.

SISTER-IN-LAW: We had nowhere else to go.

SHUI TA: There were too many of you.

WONG: What about this old couple. Were *they* parasites?

OLD MAN: We lost our shop because of you!

OLD WOMAN: And we gave your cousin money!

SHUI TA: My cousin's fiancé was a flyer. The money had to go to *him*.

WONG: Did you care whether he flew or not? Did you care whether she married him or not? You wanted her to marry someone else! [*He points at* SHU FU.]

SHUI TA: The flyer unexpectedly turned out to be a scoundrel.

YANG SUN [*jumping up*]: Which was the reason you made him your manager?

SHUI TA: Later on he improved.

WONG: And when he improved, you sold him to her? [*He points out* MRS MI TZU.]

SHUI TA: She wouldn't let me have her premises unless she had him to stroke her knees!

MRS MI TZU: What? The man's a pathological liar. [*To him*] Don't mention my property to me as long as you live! Murderer! [*She rustles off, in high dudgeon.*]

YANG SUN [*pushing in*]: My lord, I wish to speak for the defendant.

SISTER-IN-LAW: Naturally. He's your employer.

UNEMPLOYED MAN: And the worst slave driver in the country.

MRS YANG: That's a lie! My lord, Mr Shui Ta is a great man. He . . .

YANG SUN: He's this and he's that, but he is not a murderer, my lord. Just fifteen minutes before his arrest I heard Shen Te's voice in his own back room.

FIRST GOD: Oh? Tell us more!

YANG SUN: I heard sobbing, my lord!

FIRST GOD: But lots of women sob, we've been finding.

YANG SUN: Could I fail to recognize her voice?

SHU FU: No, you made her sob so often yourself, young man!

YANG SUN: Yes. But I also made her happy. Till he [*pointing at* SHUI TA] decided to sell her to you!

SHUI TA: Because you didn't love her.

WONG: Oh, no: it was for the money, my lord!

SHUI TA: And what was the money for, my lord? For the poor! And for Shen Te so she could go on being good!

WONG: For the poor? That he sent to his sweatshops? And why didn't you let Shen Te be good when you signed the big cheque?

SHUI TA: For the child's sake, my lord.

CARPENTER: What about *my* children? What did he do about them?

[SHUI TA *is silent.*]

WONG: The shop was to be a fountain of goodness. That was the gods' idea. You came and spoiled it!

SHUI TA: If I hadn't, it would have run dry!

MRS SHIN: There's a lot in that, my lord.

WONG: What have you done with the good Shen Te, bad man? She *was* good, my lords, she was, I swear it! [*He raises his hand in an oath.*]

THIRD GOD: What's happened to your hand, water seller?

WONG [*pointing to* SHUI TA]: It's all his fault, my lord, *she* was going to send me to a doctor — [*To* SHUI TA] You were her worst enemy!

SHUI TA: I was her only friend!

WONG: Where is she then? Tell us where your good friend is! [*The excitement of this exchange has run through the whole crowd.*]

ALL: Yes, where is she? Where is Shen Te? [*Etc.*]

SHUI TA: Shen Te . . . had to go.

WONG: Where? Where to?

SHUI TA: I cannot tell you! I cannot tell you!

ALL: Why? Why did she have to go away? [*Etc.*]

WONG [*into the din with the first words, but talking on beyond the others*]
Why not, why not? Why did she have to go away?

SHUI TA [*shouting*]: Because you'd all have torn her to shreds
that's why! My lords, I have a request. Clear the court! Wher
only the judges remain, I will make a confession.

ALL [*except* WONG, *who is silent, struck by the new turn of events*]
So he's guilty? He's confessing! [*Etc.*]

FIRST GOD [*using the gavel*]: Clear the court!

POLICEMAN: Clear the court!

WONG: Mr Shui Ta has met his match this time.

MRS SHIN [*with a gesture towards the judges*]: You're in for a littl
surprise.

[*The court is cleared. Silence.*]

SHUI TA: Illustrious ones!

[*The* GODS *look at each other, not quite believing their ears.*]

SHUI TA: Yes, I recognize you!

SECOND GOD [*taking matters in hand, sternly*]: What have you don
with our good woman of Setzuan?

SHUI TA: I have a terrible confession to make: I am she! [*He take.
off his mask, and tears away his clothes.* SHEN TE *stands there.*]

SECOND GOD: Shen Te!

SHEN TE: Shen Te, yes. Shui Ta *and* Shen Te. Both.

> Your injunction
> To be good and yet to live
> Was a thunderbolt:
> It has torn me in two
> I can't tell how it was
> But to be good to others
> And myself at the same time
> I could not do it

Your world is not an easy one, illustrious ones!
When we extend our hand to a beggar, he tears it off for us
When we help the lost, we are lost ourselves
And so
Since not to eat is to die
Who can long refuse to be bad?
As I lay prostrate beneath the weight of good intentions
Ruin stared me in the face
It was when I was unjust that I ate good meat
And hob-nobbed with the mighty
Why?
Why are bad deeds rewarded?
Good ones punished?
I enjoyed giving
I truly wished to be the Angel of the Slums
But washed by a foster-mother in the water of the gutter
I developed a sharp eye
The time came when pity was a thorn in my side
And, later, when kind words turned to ashes in my mouth
And anger took over
I became a wolf
Find me guilty, then, illustrious ones,
But know:
All that I have done I did
To help my neighbour
To love my lover
And to keep my little one from want
For your great, godly deeds, I was too poor, too small.

[*Pause.*]

FIRST GOD [*shocked*]: Don't go on making yourself miserable, Shen Te! We're overjoyed to have found you!

SHEN TE: I'm telling you I'm the bad man who committed all those crimes!

FIRST GOD [*using — or failing to use — his ear trumpet*]: The good woman who did all those good deeds?

SHEN TE: Yes, but the bad man too!

FIRST GOD [*as if something had dawned*]: Unfortunate coincidences! Heartless neighbours!

THIRD GOD [*shouting in his ear*]: But how is she to continue?

FIRST GOD: Continue? Well, she's a strong, healthy girl . . .

SECOND GOD: You didn't hear what she said!

FIRST GOD: I heard every word! She is confused, that's all! [*He begins to bluster*] And what about this book of rules — we can't renounce our rules, can we? [*More quietly*] Should the world be changed? How? By whom? The world should *not* be changed! [*At a sign from him, the lights turn pink, and music plays.*]

> And now the hour of parting is at hand.
> Dost thou behold, Shen Te, yon fleecy cloud?
> It is our chariot. At a sign from me
> 'Twill come and take us back from whence we came
> Above the azure vault and silver stars. . . .

SHEN TE: No! Don't go, illustrious ones!

FIRST GOD:

> Our cloud has landed now in yonder field
> From which it will transport us back to heaven.
> Farewell, Shen Te, let not thy courage fail thee. . . .

[*Exeunt* GODS.]

SHEN TE: What about the old couple? They've lost their shop? What about the water seller and his hand? And I've got to defend myself against the barber, because I don't love him! And against Sun, because I do love him! How? [SHEN TE'S *eyes follow the* GODS *as they are imagined to step into a cloud which rises and moves forward over the orchestra and up beyond the balcony.*]

FIRST GOD [*from on high*]: We have faith in you, Shen Te!

SHEN TE: There'll be a child. And he'll have to be fed. I can't stay here. Where shall I go?

FIRST GOD: Continue to be good, good woman of Setzuan!

SHEN TE: I need my bad cousin!

FIRST GOD: But not very often!

SHEN TE: Once a week at least!

FIRST GOD: Once a month will be quite enough!
SHEN TE [*shrieking*]: No, no! Help!
 [*But the cloud continues to recede as the* GODS *sing.*]

VALEDICTORY HYMN

> What rapture, oh, it is to know
>   A good thing when you see it
> And having seen a good thing, oh,
>   What rapture 'tis to flee it
>
> Be good, sweet maid of Setzuan
>   Let Shui Ta be clever
> Departing, we forget the man
>   Remember your endeavour
>
> Because through all the length of days
>   Her goodness faileth never
> Sing hallelujah! Make Shen Te's
>   Good name live on forever!

SHEN TE: Help!

*

FIRST GOD:
>   And now ... [*He makes a sign and music is heard.*
>   *Rosy light.*] let us return.
>   This little world has much engaged us.
>   Its joy and its sorrow have refreshed and pained us.
>   Up there, however, beyond the stars,
>   We shall gladly think of you, Shen Te, the good woman
>   Who bears witness to our spirit down below,
>   Who, in cold darkness, carries a little lamp!
>   Good-bye! Do it well!

[*He makes a sign and the ceiling opens. A pink cloud comes down.
On it the* THREE GODS *rise, very slowly.*]

SHEN TE: Oh, don't, illustrious ones! Don't go away! Don't leave me! How can I face the good old couple who've lost their store and the water seller with his stiff hand? And how can I defend myself from the barber whom I do not love and from Sun whom I do love? And I am with child. Soon there'll be a little son who'll want to eat. I can't stay here!

[*She turns with a hunted look toward the door which will let her tormentors in.*]

FIRST GOD: You can do it. Just be good and everything will turn out well!

[*Enter the witnesses. They look with surprise at the judges floating on their pink cloud.*]

WONG: Show respect! The gods have appeared among us!
Three of the highest gods have come to Setzuan to find a good human being. They had found one already, but . . .

FIRST GOD: No 'but'! Here she is!

ALL: Shen Te!

FIRST GOD: She has not perished. She was only hidden. She will stay with you. A good human being!

SHEN TE: But I need my cousin!

FIRST GOD: Not too often!

SHEN TE: At least once a week!

FIRST GOD: Once a month. That's enough!

SHEN TE: Oh, don't go away, illustrious ones! I haven't told you everything! I need you desperately!

[*The* GODS *sing.*]

THE TRIO OF THE VANISHING GODS
ON THE CLOUD

Unhappily we cannot stay
More than a fleeting year.
If we watch our find too long
It will disappear.

Here the golden light of truth
With shadow is alloyed
Therefore now we ask your leave
To go back to our void.

SHEN TE: Help! [*Her cries continue through the song.*]

Since our search is over now
Let us fast ascend!
The good woman of Setzuan
Praise we at the end!

[*As* SHEN TE *stretches out her arms to them in desperation, they disappear above, smiling and waving.*]

Epilogue

You're thinking, aren't you, that this is no right
Conclusion to the play you've seen tonight?
After a tale, exotic, fabulous,
A nasty ending was slipped up on us.
We feel deflated too. We too are nettled
To see the curtain down and nothing settled.
How could a better ending be arranged?
Could one change people? Can the world be changed?
Would new gods do the trick? Will atheism?
Moral rearmament? Materialism?
It is for you to find a way, my friends,
To help good men arrive at happy ends.
You write the happy ending to the play!
There must, there must, there's got to be a way!*

*When I first received the German manuscript of *Good Woman* from Brecht in 1945 it had no Epilogue. He wrote it a little later, influenced by misunderstandings of the ending in the press on the occasion of the Viennese première of the play. I believe that the Epilogue has sometimes been spoken by the actress playing Shen Te, but the actor playing Wong might be a shrewder choice, since the audience has already accepted him as a kind of chorus. On the other hand, it is not *Wong* who should deliver the Epilogue: whichever actor delivers it should drop the character he has been playing.

E.B.

QUESTIONS AND DISCUSSION POINTS

1. What would you say are the distinctive features of Brecht's style? Is it suited to his intention and message?

2. Does this piece provoke different emotions in you from the other pieces you have read? If so, in what ways are the emotions different?

3. How telling is Brecht's irony in this episode?

4. What is your opinion of the function and literary worth of the Epilogue?

5. It is often said that Brecht's plays demand a different style of acting from other plays. What style of acting do you think this extract requires?

6. Critics are deeply divided as to the literary worth of Brecht's plays. What is your own opinion? Suggest some reasons for the widely differing opinions which are current.

ARTHUR MILLER

Death of a Salesman

Death of a Salesman (1949) is the play in which Arthur Miller reached the height of his powers and established himself as one of America's leading playwrights. The play examines the failure of a commercial 'little man' to realize his modest ambitions of social stability and popularity, relating this personal tragedy very subtly to an acutely analysed milieu of remorseless commercialism.

The play begins with Willy Loman, a sixty-three-year-old salesman, on the point of a nervous crisis, no longer able to face up to the increasingly thankless task of trying to sell his line to stores which are less and less easily lured by the salestalk of the once ebullient but now pathetic salesman. Nor is he able to face up to the physical strain of long drives to and from his traditional sales 'territory', New England. His wife, Linda, is anxiously sympathetic, loving him realistically and tolerating the pretence and self-deception which he has acquired in forty years of selling. His sons, Happy, who lives at home, and Biff, at present paying one of his infrequent visits, have a less sympathetic attitude. Biff particularly, disillusioned, as we learn, by his discovery as a schoolboy of his father's infidelity, is cynically bitter towards the conscience-stricken Willy whom he had once adored. Of the earlier happy family relationships we learn a good deal through a series of flash-backs to the days when Willy was the happy, confident father of two boisterously confident and successful sons. The clash between Biff and his father, with Linda acting as peace-maker, is one of the central features of the play and is made more tragic and convincing by the frequent unavailing efforts of both to find some sort of *modus vivendi*.

Another vitally important character is 'Uncle Ben', Willy's brother, who has attained the kind of success of which Willy has only dreamed and who is presented as an adventurous, pioneering type: 'When I was seventeen I walked into the jungle and when I was twenty-one I walked out. (He laughs.) And by God I was rich.' He makes this claim in one of the several flash-back scenes in which he appears. As the play progresses, Willy increasingly finds solace in these reminiscences and in his preparations for his contemplated suicide. Willy's degeneration is commented on by a wryly sane and commonsense neighbour, Charley.

At last, confronted by Biff with the unpalatable truth which his job as a salesman has enabled him to hide under a welter of spurious popularity, Willy takes the ultimate step of retreat, committing suicide, hoping that he will at least give his family enough to see them through, the insurance. To the last, Willy clings on to his naïve ideals of opportunity for all, as embodied by Uncle Ben, and refuses to accept the precocious wisdom of Biff:

WILLY [*with hatred, threateningly*]: The door of your life is wide open!

BIFF: Pop! I'm a dime a dozen, and so are you!

WILLY [*turning on him now in an uncontrolled outburst*]: I am not a dime a dozen! I am Willy Loman, and you are Biff Loman!

At this stage, the truth is dangerously close, too close for Willy, and he opts out of a life which has used him and which has now cast him aside — the scene in which he is rejected by his employer is wonderfully moving — giving rise to the choric summary of Charley on the nature of Willy's life as a salesman, and on the whole commercial way of life: 'And then you get yourself a couple of spots on your hat, and you're finished . . . A salesman is got to dream boy. It comes with the territory.'

The greatness of the play is that it shows the tragic human waste involved in the inhuman rejection by the commercial system of someone who has degraded himself in serving it, but who has retained sufficient sense of human worth and dignity not to want to believe the harsh truth.

       ★   ★   ★   ★   ★

This is a crucial episode of the play, beginning as it does with Biff's discovery of his father's infidelity while away from home on business trips. The episode illustrates the 'flash-back' technique by which Miller succeeds in showing the gradual crumbling of a happy past into a pitiful and helpless present. Willy recalls the painful and traumatic scene of discovery in a hotel room, after being left in a restaurant by Biff and Happy. Returning home, Biff and Happy are met by the now thoroughly roused Linda, and they see the pitiful state to which Willy is now reduced. Biff has sought out his father in the hope that Willy may be able to persuade a teacher to give Biff the marks he needs to qualify for a University course. As the episode begins, Willy has just chased the woman out of his room. The entrance of Stanley later takes us back to the restaurant.

Extract from *Death of a Salesman*

Pp. 94–101 of Penguin edition.

(First published by the Cresset Press)

WILLY [*after a pause*]: Well, better get going. I want to get to the school first thing in the morning. Get my suits out of the closet. I'll get my valise. [BIFF *doesn't move.*] What's the matter? [BIFF *remains motionless, tears falling.*] She's a buyer. Buys for J. H. Simmons. She lives down the hall — they're painting. You don't imagine — [*He breaks off. After a pause.*] Now listen, pal, she's just a buyer. She sees merchandise in her room and they have to keep it looking just so . . . [*Pause. Assuming command.*] All right, get my suits. [BIFF *doesn't move.*] Now stop crying and do as I say. I gave you an order. Biff, I gave you an order! Is that what you do when I give you an order? How dare you cry? [*Putting his arm around* BIFF.] Now look, Biff, when you grow up you'll understand about these things. You mustn't — you mustn't over-emphasize a thing like this. I'll see Birnbaum first thing in the morning.

BIFF: Never mind.

WILLY [*getting down beside* BIFF]: Never mind! He's going to give you those points. I'll see to it.

BIFF: He wouldn't listen to you.

WILLY: He certainly will listen to me. You need those points for the U. of Virginia.

BIFF: I'm not going there.

WILLY: Heh? If I can't get him to change that mark you'll make it up in summer school. You've got all summer to —

BIFF [*his weeping breaking from him*]: Dad . . .

WILLY [*infected by it*]: Oh, my boy . . .

BIFF: Dad . . .

WILLY: She's nothing to me, Biff. I was lonely, I was terribly lonely.

BIFF: You — you gave her Mama's stockings! [*His tears break through and he rises to go.*]

WILLY [*grabbing for* BIFF]: I gave you an order!

BIFF: Don't touch me, you — liar!

WILLY: Apologize for that!

BIFF: You fake! You phony little fake! You fake! [*Overcome he turns quickly and weeping fully goes out with his suitcase.* WILLY *is left on the floor on his knees.*]

WILLY: I gave you an order! Biff, come back here or I'll beat you! Come back here! I'll whip you!

[STANLEY *comes quickly in from the right and stands in front of* WILLY.]

WILLY [*shouts at* STANLEY]: I gave you an order . . .

STANLEY: Hey, let's pick it up, pick it up, Mr Loman. [*He helps* WILLY *to his feet.*] Your boys left with the chippies. They said they'll see you home.

[*A second waiter watches some distance away.*]

WILLY: But we were supposed to have dinner together.

[*Music is heard,* WILLY'*s theme.*]

STANLEY: Can you make it?

WILLY: I'll — sure, I can make it. [*Suddenly concerned about his clothes.*] Do I — I look all right?

STANLEY: Sure, you look all right. [*He flicks a speck off* WILLY'S *lapel.*]

WILLY: Here — here's a dollar.

STANLEY: Oh, your son paid me. It's all right.

WILLY [*putting it in* STANLEY'S *hand*]: No, take it. You're a good boy.

STANLEY: Oh, no, you don't have to . . .

WILLY: Here — here's some more. I don't need it any more. [*After a slight pause.*] Tell me — is there a seed store in the neighbourhood?

STANLEY: Seeds? You mean like to plant?

[*As* WILLY *turns,* STANLEY *slips the money back into his jacket pocket.*]

WILLY: Yes. Carrots, peas . . .

STANLEY: Well, there's hardware stores on Sixth Avenue, but it may be too late now.

WILLY [*anxiously*]: Oh, I'd better hurry. I've got to get some seeds. [*He starts off to the right.*] I've got to get some seeds, right away. Nothing's planted. I don't have a thing in the ground.

[WILLY *hurries out as the light goes down.* STANLEY *moves over to the right after him, watches him off. The other waiter has been staring at* WILLY.]

STANLEY [*to the waiter*]: Well, whatta you looking at?

[*The waiter picks up the chairs and moves off right.*

STANLEY *takes the table and follows him. The light fades on this area. There is a long pause, the sound of the flute coming over. The light gradually rises on the kitchen, which is empty.* HAPPY *appears at the door of the house, followed by* BIFF. HAPPY *is carrying a large bunch of long-stemmed roses. He enters the kitchen, looks around for* LINDA. *Not seeing her, he turns to* BIFF, *who is just outside the house door, and makes a gesture with his hands, indicating 'Not here, I guess'. He looks into the living-room and freezes. Inside,* LINDA, *unseen, is seated,* WILLY'S *coat on her lap. She rises ominously and quietly and moves towards* HAPPY, *who backs up into the kitchen, afraid.*]

HAPPY: Hey, what're you doing up? [LINDA *says nothing but moves toward him implacably.*] Where's Pop? [*He keeps backing to the right, and now* LINDA *is in full view in the doorway to the living-room.*] Is he sleeping?

LINDA: Where were you?

HAPPY [*trying to laugh it off*]: We met two girls, Mom, very fine types. Here, we brought you some flowers. [*Offering them to her.*] Put them in your room, Ma. [*She knocks them to the floor at* BIFF's *feet. He has now come inside and closed the door behind him. She stares at* BIFF, *silent.*]

HAPPY: Now what'd you do that for? Mom, I want you to have some flowers —

LINDA [*cutting* HAPPY *off, violently to* BIFF]: Don't you care whether he lives or dies?

HAPPY [*going to the stairs*]: Come upstairs, Biff.

BIFF [*with a flare of disgust, to* HAPPY]: Go away from me! [*To* LINDA.] What do you mean, lives or dies? Nobody's dying around here, pal.

LINDA: Get out of my sight! Get out of here!

BIFF: I wanna see the boss.

LINDA: You're not going near him!

BIFF: Where is he? [*He moves into the living-room and* LINDA *follows.*]

LINDA [*shouting after* BIFF]: You invite him to dinner. He looks forward to it all day — [BIFF *appears in his parents' bedroom, looks around, and exits*] — and then you desert him there. There's no stranger you'd do that to!

HAPPY: Why, he had a swell time with us. Listen, when I — [LINDA *comes back into the kitchen*] — desert him I hope I don't outlive the day.

LINDA: Get out of here!

HAPPY: Now look, Mom . . .

LINDA: Did you have to go to women tonight? You and your lousy rotten whores!

[BIFF *re-enters the kitchen.*]

HAPPY: Mom, all we did was follow Biff around trying to cheer him up! [*To* BIFF.] Boy, what a night you gave me!

LINDA: Get out of here, both of you, and don't come back! I don't want you tormenting him any more. Go on now, get your things together! [*To* BIFF.] You can sleep in his apartment. [*She starts to pick up the flowers and stops herself.*] Pick up this stuff, I'm not your maid any more. Pick it up, you bum, you!

[HAPPY *turns his back to her in refusal.* BIFF *slowly moves over and gets down on his knees, picking up the flowers.*]

LINDA: You're a pair of animals! Not one, not another living soul would have had the cruelty to walk out on that man in a restaurant!

BIFF [*not looking at her*]: Is that what he said?

LINDA: He didn't have to say anything. He was so humiliated he nearly limped when he came in.

HAPPY: But, Mom, he had a great time with us —

BIFF [*cutting him off violently*]: Shut up!

[*Without another word,* HAPPY *goes upstairs.*]

LINDA: You didn't even go in to see if he was all right!

BIFF [*still on the floor in front of* LINDA, *the flowers in his hand; with self-loathing*]: No. Didn't do a damned thing. How do you like that, heh? Left him babbling in a toilet.

LINDA: You louse. You . . .

BIFF: Now you hit it on the nose! [*Gets up, throws the flowers in the wastebasket.*] The scum of the earth, and you're looking at him!

LINDA: Get out of here!

BIFF: I gotta talk to the boss, Mom. Where is he?

LINDA: You're not going near him. Get out of this house!

BIFF [*with absolute assurance, determination*]: No. We're gonna have an abrupt conversation, him and me.

LINDA: You're not talking to him!

[*Hammering is heard from outside the house, off right.* BIFF *turns toward the noise.*]

LINDA [*suddenly pleading*]: Will you please leave him alone?

BIFF: What's he doing out there?

LINDA: He's planting the garden!

BIFF [*quietly*]: Now? Oh, my God!

[BIFF *moves outside,* LINDA *following. The light dies down on them and comes up on the centre of the apron as* WILLY *walks into it. He is carrying a flashlight, a hoe and a handful of seed packets. He raps the top of the hoe sharply to fix it firmly, and then moves to the left, measuring off the distance with his foot. He holds the flashlight to look at the seed packets, reading off the instructions. He is in the blue of night.*]

WILLY: Carrots . . . quarter-inch apart. Rows . . . one-foot rows. [*He measures it off.*] One foot. [*He puts down a package and measures off.*] Beets. [*He puts down another package and measures again.*] Lettuce. [*He reads the package puts it down.*] One foot — [*He breaks off as* BEN *appears at the right and moves slowly down to him.*] What a proposition, ts, ts. Terrific, terrific. 'Cause she's suffered, Ben, the woman has suffered. You understand me? A man can't go out the way he came in, Ben, a man has got to add up to something. You can't, you can't — [BEN *moves toward him as though to interrupt.*] You gotta consider, now. Don't answer so quick. Remember, it's a guaranteed twenty-thousand-dollar proposition. Now look, Ben, I want you to go through the ins and outs of this thing with me. I've got nobody to talk to, Ben, and the woman has suffered, you hear me?

BEN [*standing still, considering*]: What's the proposition?

WILLY: It's twenty thousand dollars on the barrelhead. Guaranteed, gilt-edged, you understand?

BEN: You don't want to make a fool of yourself. They might not honour the policy.

WILLY: How can they dare refuse? Didn't I work like a coolie to meet every premium on the nose? And now they don't pay off! Impossible!

BEN: It's called a cowardly thing, William.

WILLY: Why? Does it take more guts to stand here the rest of my life ringing up a zero?

BEN [*yielding*]: That's a point, William. [*He moves, thinking, turns.*] And twenty thousand — that is something one can feel with the hand, it is there.

WILLY [*now assured, with rising power*]: Oh, Ben, that's the whole beauty of it! I see it like a diamond, shining in the dark, hard and rough, that I can pick up and touch in my hand. Not like — like an appointment! This would not be another damned-fool appointment, Ben, and it changes all the aspects. Because he thinks I'm nothing, see, and so he spites me. But the funeral — [*straightening up*] Ben, that funeral will be massive! They'll come from Maine, Massachusetts, Vermont, New Hampshire! All the old-timers with the strange licence plates — that boy will be thunderstruck, Ben, because he never realized — I am known! Rhode Island, New York, New Jersey — I am known, Ben, and he'll see it with his eyes once and for all. He'll see what I am, Ben! He's in for a shock, that boy!

BEN [*coming down to the edge of the garden*]: He'll call you a coward.

WILLY [*suddenly fearful*]: No, that would be terrible.

BEN: Yes. And a damned fool.

WILLY: No, no, he mustn't, I won't have that! [*He is broken and desperate.*]

BEN: He'll hate you, William.

[*The gay music of the boys is heard.*]

WILLY: Oh, Ben, how do we get back to all the great times? Used to be so full of light, and comradeship, the sleigh-riding in winter, and the ruddiness on his cheeks. And always some kind of good news coming up, always something nice coming up ahead. And never even let me carry the valises in the house, and simonizing that little red car! Why, why can't I give him something and not have him hate me?

QUESTIONS AND DISCUSSION POINTS

1. How does Miller enlist our sympathy for Willy?
2. Do you think the flash-back technique successful?
3. How does Miller gain our sympathy for Biff?
4. How would you describe the state of mind of the main characters in this episode?
5. Does the way in which the characters speak reveal their personalities and moods?
6. Is Willy Loman a genuinely tragic figure? Or is he merely pathetic?

ARNOLD WESKER

Roots

Roots, first performed in May, 1959, is the second play in the Wesker *Trilogy*, which comprises *Chicken Soup with Barley*, *Roots* and *I'm Talking about Jerusalem*. These three plays trace the development of a group of people, centring on the Kahn family, from pre-war poverty to post-war affluence, the unifying theme being the relation between Socialism and this changing society. The central figure of the *Trilogy* is the son of the Kahn family, Ronnie.

Although he does not appear physically in *Roots*, Ronnie and his beliefs are a very powerful presence in the play. The main character of *Roots* is Beatie Bryant, the daughter of a Norfolk farming family, who has met Ronnie Kahn while in London; they intend to marry. Beatie has been deeply influenced by Ronnie's political and cultural beliefs and returning to her home tries to convert her family to these beliefs, tries, in fact, to preach Socialism to those for whom it is intended. The play, then, has two major themes; the relationship between Beatie and her family as it is affected by her love for Ronnie; and the relevance of Socialism to rural working class life.

As the play opens, Beatie, having returned home to prepare for a visit from Ronnie, is telling her family, rather smugly, how much she has learned from Ronnie and is trying to convert them to her, or rather Ronnie's, way of thinking. The response is good-natured apathy at first but later a trace of resentment begins to show itself, and justifiably so, for the views that Beatie is trying to communicate at this stage are merely a garbled version of Ronnie's.

We see pretty clearly that at this stage Beatie's Socialism is merely a matter of ill-digested platitudes. We also see, however, that the people to whom she is preaching are in need of some kind of vitalizing impulse; their lives are seen to be largely a matter of satisfying animal wants; their emotions, as they express them, are crudely monotonous. 'As they express them,' is important because Wesker never doubts that these people have powerful emotions and great human potential; their lack of awareness and their linguistic inadequacy prevent the realization of this potential. Beatie herself represents the possibility of development which is theirs for the taking if they will make the initial effort to re-examine their lives. At this stage, of course, Beatie's development is by no means complete, but she is at least trying.

The tragic waste of rural working class life is exemplified as the play proceeds by the stupid, pointless death of the local drunk, Stan Mann, and the Bryant family's acceptance of this tragedy as inevitable and unavoidable. The shabby treatment meted out to Beatie's father by his employer further exemplifies the rural working class's need for the words with which to express themselves and secure their rights. The first two acts of the play centre on the relationship between Beatie and her mother and show clearly the deficiencies of both sides. Beatie is trying, however crudely, to show her mother what she has learned from Ronnie and her mother responds sometimes resentfully and reproachfully and sometimes patiently and helpfully. No real progress is being made, however. An impasse has been reached between Beatie and her family, and a crisis is needed to precipitate further development.

This crisis occurs when Ronnie ends his relationship with Beatie. He tells Beatie of this decision in a letter which arrives at her home on the day he is expected. Beatie's reaction to this blow is the crux of the play. She responds positively. No longer able to rely on Ronnie she nevertheless realizes that what he has told her has a validity which is independent of her personal feeling towards him. No longer able to preface almost every remark with 'Ronnie says' she realizes for herself that what she has learned from Ronnie is vitally relevant to the life of her family, a life whose emotions are being blunted and cheapened by mass culture, in the absence of the education which would enable them to think for themselves. In spite of the jeers of her mother, she sees her way into the future; she has begun now to think for herself; the way is open, through her, for the social class in which she has her roots. The roots have been nourished and have begun to grow for themselves and what has happened for Beatie, Wesker is saying, could happen for a whole class.

In this play Wesker has managed to overcome the fundamental difficulty which faces the 'social' dramatist; he has made his social point through the powerful exploration of an individual's development. He has managed to suggest the wider relevance of an individual case rather than merely present a prosaic example of his social viewpoint.

       ★   ★   ★   ★   ★

The episode which follows occurs at the end of Act Two and shows Beatie trying to widen her mother's cultural interests with rather tactless enthusiasm. The undertones of impatience on Beatie's part, and resentment on her mother's, point towards the rift which occurs in the final act. As the episode begins, Beatie is having a bath behind a screen in the living room.

Extract from *Roots*

Pp. 54–58 of Penguin edition.

BEATIE: Mother, what we gonna make Ronnie when he come?

MRS BRYANT: Well, what do he like?

BEATIE: He like trifle and he like steak and kidney pie.

MRS BRYANT: We'll make that then. So long as he don't complain o' the guts ache. Frankie hev it too sometimes and Jenny's husband James.

BEATIE: Know why? You all eat too much. The Londoners think we live a healthy life but they don't know we stuff ourselves silly till our guts ache. Look at that lunch we had. Lamb chops, spuds, runner beans, and three Yorkshire puddings.

MRS BRYANT: But you know what's wrong wi' Jimmy Beales? It's indigestion. He eat too fast.

BEATIE: What the hell's indigestion doin' a'tween his shoulder blades?

MRS BRYANT: 'Cos some people get it so bad it go right through their stomach to the back.

BEATIE: You don't get indigestion in the back mother, what you on about?

MRS BRYANT: Don't you tell me gal, I hed it!

BEATIE: Owee! The soap's in my eyes — mother, towel, the towel, quickly the towel!

[MRS BRYANT *hands in towel to* BEATIE. *The washing up is probably done by now, so* MRS BRYANT *sits in a chair, legs apart and arms folded thinking what else to say.*]

MRS BRYANT: You heard that Ma Buckley hev been taken to Mental Hospital in Norwich? Poor ole dear. If there's one thing I can't abide that's mental cases. They frighten me — they do. Can't face 'em. I'd sooner follow a man to a churchyard than the mental hospital. That's a terrible thing to see a person lose their reason — that 'tis. Well, I tell you what, down where I used to live, down the other side of the Hall, years ago we moved in next to an old woman. I only had Jenny and Frank then — an' this

106

woman she were the sweetest of people. We used to talk and do errands for each other — Oh she was a sweet ole dear. And then one afternoon I was going out to get my washin' in and I saw her. She was standin' in a tub o' water up to her neck. She was! Up to her neck. An' her eyes had that glazed, wonderin' look and she stared straight at me she did. Straight at me. Well, do you know what? I was struck *dumb*. I was *struck* dumb wi' shock. What wi' her bein' so nice all this while, the sudden comin' on her like that in the tub fair upset me. It did! And people tell me afterwards that she's bin goin' in an' out o' hospital for years. Blust, that scare me. That scare me so much she nearly took me round the bend wi' her.

[BEATIE *appears from behind the curtain in her dressing-gown and a towel round her head.*]

BEATIE: There! I'm gonna hev a bath every day when I'm married.

[BEATIE *starts rubbing her hair with towel and fiddles with radio. She finds a programme playing Mendelssohn's 4th Symphony.* MRS BRYANT *unhitches the curtains, folds them up, and then they both lift up the bath and take it off into the garden. When they return* MRS BRYANT *replaces the displaced furniture while* BEATIE *rubs her hair and stands before the mirror.*]

BEATIE [*looking at her reflection*]: Isn't your nose a funny thing, and your ears; and your arms and your legs, aren't they funny things — sticking out of a lump.

MRS BRYANT [*switching off radio*]: Turn that squit off!

BEATIE [*turning on her mother violently*]: MOTHER! I could kill you when you do that. No wonder I don't know anything about anything. You give me nothing that was worthwhile, nothing. I never knowed anything about the news because you always switched off after the headlines. I never read any good books 'cos there was never any in the house. I never heard nothing but dance music because you always turned off the classics. I can't even speak English proper because you never talked about anything important.

MRS BRYANT: What's gotten into you now gal?

BEATIE: God in heaven mother, you live in the country but you got no — no — no majesty. You spend your time among green fields, you grow flowers and you breathe fresh air and you got no majesty. You go on and you go on talking and talking so your mind's cluttered up with nothing and you shut out the world. What kind of a life did you give me?

MRS BRYANT: Blust gal, I weren't no teacher.

BEATIE: But you hindered. You didn't open one door for me. Even his [*Ronnie's*] mother cared more for me than what you did. Beatie, she say, Beatie, why don't you take up evening classes and learn something other than waitressing. Yes, she say, you won't ever regret learnin' things. But did you care what job I took up or whether I learned things. You didn't even think it was necessary.

MRS BRYANT: I fed you. I clothed you. I took you out to the sea. What more d'you want. We're only country folk you know. We ent got no big things here you know.

BEATIE: Squit! Squit! It makes no difference country or town. *All* the town girls I ever worked with were just like me. It makes no difference country or town — that's squit. Do you know when I used to work at the holiday camp and I sat down with the other girls to write a letter we used to sit and discuss what we wrote about. An' we all agreed, all on us, that we started: 'Just a few lines to let you know,' and then we get on to the weather and then we get stuck so we write about each other and after a page an' half of big scrawl end up: 'Hoping this finds you as well as it leaves me.' There! We couldn't say any more. Thousands of things happening at this holiday camp and we couldn't find words for them. All of us the same. Hundreds of girls and one day we're gonna be mothers, and you *still* talk to me of Jimmy Skelton and the ole woman in the tub. Do you know I've heard that story a dozen times. A dozen times. Don't you know what you're talking about? Jesus, how can I bring Ronnie to this house.

MRS BRYANT: Blust gal, if Ronnie don't like us then he —

BEATIE: Oh, he'll like you alright. He like most people. He'd've loved ole Stan Mann. Old Stan Mann would've understood everything Ronnie talk about. Blust! That man liked livin'.

Besides, Ronnie say it's too late for the old uns to learn. But he says it's up to us young 'uns. And them of us that know hev got to take them of us as don't know and bloody well teach them.

MRS BRYANT: I bet he hev a hard job changing you gal!

BEATIE: He's *not* trying to change me mother. You can't change people, he say, you can only give them some love and hope they'll take it. And that's what he's tryin' to do with me and I'm tryin' to understand — do you see that mother?

MRS BRYANT: I don't see what that's got to do with music though.

BEATIE: Oh my God! [*Suddenly.*] I'll show you. [*Goes off to front room to collect pick-up and a record.*] Now sit you down gal and I'll show you. Don't start ironing or reading or nothing, just sit there and be prepared to learn something. [*Appears with pick-up and switches in.*] You aren't too old, just you sit and listen. That's the trouble you see, we ent ever prepared to learn anything, we close our minds the minute anything unfamiliar appear. *I* could never listen to music. I used to like some on it but then I'd lose patience, I'd go to bed in the middle of a symphony, or my mind would wander 'cos the music didn't mean anything to me so I'd go to bed or start talking. 'Christ almighty,' he'd say, 'don't you know something's happening around you? Aren't you aware of something that's bigger'n you? Sit back woman,' he'd say, 'listen to it. Let it happen to you and you'll grow as big as the music itself.'

MRS BRYANT: Blust he talk like a book.

BEATIE: An' sometimes he talk as though you didn't know where the moon or the stars was. [BEATIE *puts on record of Bizet's 'L'Arlesienne Suite'*.] Now listen. This is a simple piece of music, it's not highbrow but it's full of living. You want to dance to it. And that's what he say Socialism is. 'Christ,' he say, 'Socialism isn't talking all the time, it's living, it's singing, it's dancing, it's being interested in what go on around you, it's being concerned about people and the world.' Listen mother. [*She becomes breathless and excited.*] Listen to it. It's simple isn't it. Can you call that squit?

MRS BRYANT: I don't say it's all squit.

BEATIE: You don't have to frown because it's alive.

MRS BRYANT: No, not all on it's squit.

BEATIE: See the way the other tune comes in? Hear it? Two simple tunes, one after the other.

MRS BRYANT: I aren't saying it's all squit.

BEATIE: And now listen, listen, it goes together, the two tunes together, they knit, they're perfect. Don't it make you want to dance? [*She begins to dance a mixture of a cossack dance and a sailor's hornpipe.*]

[*The music becomes fast and her spirits are young and high.*]

Listen to that mother. Is it difficult? Is it squit? It's light. It make me feel light and confident and happy. God mother we could all be so much more alive and happy. Wheeeee . . .

[BEATIE *claps her hands and dances and her* MOTHER *smiles and claps her hands and —*]

THE CURTAIN FALLS

QUESTIONS AND DISCUSSION POINTS

1. Does Wesker succeed in showing sympathetically the virtues and shortcomings of both Beatie and her mother?

2. How does Wesker avoid the danger of preaching?

3. What do the prosaic details and gossip add to the total effect?

4. Is Wesker successful in catching the different speech habits of Beatie and her mother?

5. Is the final elation dramatically effective?

6. What does this episode add to the play's theme as sketched in the introduction to the extract?

THE THEATRE OF THE ABSURD

SAMUEL BECKETT

Waiting for Godot

THE Peter Hall production of *Waiting for Godot* in 1955 has been seen by some critics as a great landmark in the history of the English theatre; by others as just one more example of the literary anarchy of this century. Beckett's later plays have made the initial conflict of opinion even sharper and more fierce, and indeed his development since *Godot* makes the earlier play seem almost traditional in its methods and hopeful in its philosophy. A recent work, *Play*, indeed, denies his characters the power of movement completely, and consists of one act which is repeated to form the second act. At a distance of almost ten years, it is now possible, with the help of the few perceptive pieces of criticism about the play, to see it as being a coherent dramatic statement of Beckett's view of the human condition.

The play conveys its message by an extension of the dramatic methods introduced by such dramatists as Strindberg, Chekhov and Pirandello. There is no narrative sequence; meaning emerges only fitfully from the apparently inconsequential dialogue; apparently pointless remarks take on metaphysical overtones by being repeated in different situations; the conclusion is inconclusive.

Two pathetic figures, possibly tramps though even this is not stated, wait, beside a tree, for a mysterious figure with whom, Vladimir asserts and Estragon believes, they have an appointment. The name of this mysterious figure, who they feel will in some way

change their lives, is Godot. They do not know the time or place
of this appointment, nor do they know what Godot looks like.
Nevertheless, Vladimir strongly believes that he has indeed such an
appointment and Estragon has neither the energy nor wit to
contradict him, though he occasionally expresses a rather spiteful
scepticism which thoroughly disconcerts Vladimir. While they
wait, they reminisce, reflect and argue, and their thoughts and
words reveal their past life to be meaningless, to be a matter for
mild regret merely. They both try to evade this truth, and Vladimir
in particular hopes that Godot is going to give their lives a purpose
and a meaning. Vladimir, disturbed by doubts as to the authenticity
of the Bible narrative of the Redemption, maintains hope only by
ignoring certain areas of experience: 'Don't tell me,' he yells when
Estragon proposes to narrate one of his dreams. Dreams, perhaps,
represent the innate evil of life which Vladimir must ignore, or at
least they are uncontrollable and therefore disturbing. Beckett's
great achievement in the play is to suggest the universality of the
state represented by Vladimir and Estragon.

A concrete example of man's desperate retreat from the unpleasant truth is the reaction of Vladimir and Estragon to the
enigmatic pair, Pozzo and Lucky. Pozzo treats Lucky more cruelly
than he would an animal. One tenable interpretation of the meaning
of the pair is that Pozzo represents mankind, and Lucky Christ. If
this view is accepted, what takes place before Vladimir and Estragon
is the re-acting of the Redemption. Vladimir and Estragon, of
course, do not recognize it as such, find it unpleasant, and prefer to
continue waiting for the vague Godot. Faced by what they have
ostensibly been waiting for, they find the truth unpleasant and
therefore reject it. Another possible interpretation of this episode
is that Pozzo and Lucky represent human life, Pozzo representing
the physical aspect of the human personality and Lucky the spiritual,
which is in time brutalized by the treatment it receives and is
reduced to the incoherence represented in the play by Lucky's
outburst when his 'thinking hat' is put on his head. Pozzo himself
in the course of the play turns blind, this perhaps being an indication
of the transience of human power and domination. Seeing Pozzo

blind, Vladimir tries to fit this fact into a time scheme which might in some way explain it. Pozzo rages back at him:

> Have you not done tormenting me with your accursed time? It's abominable. When! When! One day, is that not enough for you, one day like any other day, one day he [Lucky] went dumb, one day I went blind, one day we'll go deaf, one day we were born, one day we'll die, the same day, the same second, is that not enough for you? [*Calmer*.] They give birth astride of a grave, the light gleams an instant, then it's night once more.

Such a passage shows why this is not just a depressing play; the stark view of life is transmuted by the creative energy with which it is communicated.

Vladimir, the searcher after a kind of truth, has an inkling of what all this means, but hurriedly reverts to his former comfortably vague optimism in which tomorrow will be a better day rather than simply part of the agonizingly persistent human tragedy represented by Pozzo and Lucky. The play ends with Godot's 'messenger', a boy — who represents perhaps conventional religion — and his promise that Godot will come tomorrow. Even a final effort by Estragon to do something, even though it is merely to hang himself, ends with the absurdity of his trousers falling down after he has removed the rope which had served as a belt, but which, Vladimir says, is too short for a hanging rope. Things are as they were; Vladimir and Estragon have staved off reality and truth for another day.

Into this wonderfully suggestive and subtle play, Beckett incorporates such minor themes as the inadequacy of human language as a means of communication and the illusory nature of such concepts as past and future, the whole having the universal relevance which only a poet can give to an otherwise unremarkable situation.

*　　*　　*　　*　　*

The following extract shows the beginning of the encounter between Vladimir and Estragon, and Pozzo and Lucky.

F

Extract from *Waiting for Godot*

Pp. 19–26 of Faber edition.

VLADIMIR [*raising his hand*]: Listen!
  [*They listen, grotesquely rigid.*]
ESTRAGON: I hear nothing.
VLADIMIR: Hssst! [*They listen.* ESTRAGON *loses his balance, almost falls. He clutches the arm of* VLADIMIR, *who totters. They listen, huddled together.*] Nor I.
  [*Sighs of relief. They relax and separate.*]
ESTRAGON: You gave me a fright.
VLADIMIR: I thought it was he.
ESTRAGON: Who?
VLADIMIR: Godot.
ESTRAGON: Pah! The wind in the reeds.
VLADIMIR: I could have sworn I heard shouts.
ESTRAGON: And why would he shout?
VLADIMIR: At his horse. [*Silence.*]
ESTRAGON: I'm hungry.
VLADIMIR: Do you want a carrot?
ESTRAGON: Is that all there is?
VLADIMIR: I might have some turnips.
ESTRAGON: Give me a carrot. [*Vladimir rummages in his pockets, takes out a turnip and gives it to* ESTRAGON *who takes a bite out of it. Angrily.*] It's a turnip!
VLADIMIR: O pardon! I could have sworn it was a carrot. [*He rummages again in his pockets, finds nothing but turnips.*] All that's turnips. [*He rummages.*] You must have eaten the last. [*He rummages.*] Wait, I have it. [*He brings out a carrot and gives it to* ESTRAGON.] There, dear fellow. [ESTRAGON *wipes it on his sleeve and begins to eat it.*] Make it last; that's the end of them.
ESTRAGON [*chewing*]: I asked you a question.
VLADIMIR: Ah!
ESTRAGON: Did you reply?
VLADIMIR: How's the carrot?

116

ESTRAGON: It's a carrot.

VLADIMIR: So much the better, so much the better. [*Pause.*] What was it you wanted to know?

ESTRAGON: I've forgotten. [*Chews.*] That's what annoys me. [*He looks at the carrot appreciatively, dangles it between finger and thumb.*] I'll never forget this carrot. [*He sucks the end of it meditatively.*] Ah yes, now I remember.

VLADIMIR: Well?

ESTRAGON [*his mouth full, vacuously*]: We're not tied?

VLADIMIR: I don't hear a word you're saying.

ESTRAGON [*chews, swallows*]: I'm asking you if we're tied.

VLADIMIR: Tied?

ESTRAGON: Ti-ed.

VLADIMIR: How do you mean tied?

ESTRAGON: Down.

VLADIMIR: But by whom. By whom?

ESTRAGON: To your man.

VLADIMIR: To Godot? Tied to Godot? What an idea! No question of it.
[*Pause.*] For the moment.

ESTRAGON: His name is Godot?

VLADIMIR: I think so.

ESTRAGON: Fancy that. [*He raises what remains of the carrot by the stub of leaf, twirls it before his eyes.*] Funny, the more you eat the worse it gets.

VLADIMIR: With me it's just the opposite.

ESTRAGON: In other words?

VLADIMIR: I get used to the muck as I go along.

ESTRAGON [*after prolonged reflection*]: Is that the opposite?

VLADIMIR: Question of temperament.

ESTRAGON: Of character.

VLADIMIR: Nothing you can do about it.

ESTRAGON: No use struggling.

VLADIMIR: One is what one is.

ESTRAGON: No use wriggling.

VLADIMIR: The essential doesn't change.

ESTRAGON: Nothing to be done. [*He proffers the remains of the carrot to* VLADIMIR.] Like to finish it?

[*A terrible cry, close at hand.* ESTRAGON *drops the carrot. They remain motionless, then together make a sudden rush towards the wings.* ESTRAGON *stops half-way, runs back, picks up the carrot, stuffs it in his pocket, runs towards* VLADIMIR, *who is waiting for him, stops again, runs back, picks up his boot, runs to rejoin* VLADIMIR. *Huddled together, shoulders hunched, cringing away from the menace, they wait.*

Enter POZZO *and* LUCKY. POZZO *drives* LUCKY *by means of a rope passed round his neck, so that* LUCKY *is the first to appear, followed by the rope, which is long enough to allow him to reach the middle of the stage before* POZZO *appears,* LUCKY *carries a heavy bag, a folding stool, a picnic basket and a greatcoat.* POZZO *a whip.*]

POZZO [*off*]: On! [*Crack of whip.* POZZO *appears. They cross the stage.* LUCKY *passes before* VLADIMIR *and* ESTRAGON *and exits.* POZZO *at the sight of* VLADIMIR *and* ESTRAGON *stops short. The rope tautens.* POZZO *jerks it violently.*] Back! [*Noise of* LUCKY *falling with all his baggage.* VLADIMIR *and* ESTRAGON *turn towards him, divided between the wish to go to his assistance and the fear of not minding their own business.* VLADIMIR *takes a step towards* LUCKY, ESTRAGON *holds him back by the sleeves.*]

VLADIMIR: Let me go!

ESTRAGON: Stay where you are!

POZZO: Be careful! He's wicked. [VLADIMIR *and* ESTRAGON *turn towards* POZZO.] With strangers.

ESTRAGON [*undertone*]: Is that him?

VLADIMIR: Who?

ESTRAGON [*trying to remember the name*]: Er . . .

VLADIMIR: Godot?

ESTRAGON: Yes.

POZZO: I present myself: Pozzo.

VLADIMIR [*to* ESTRAGON]: Not at all!

ESTRAGON [*timidly to* POZZO]: You're not Mr. Godot, sir?

POZZO [*terrifying voice*]: I am Pozzo! [*Silence.*] Pozzo!

[*Silence.*] Does that name mean nothing to you? [*Silence.*]

[*Silence.*] I say does that name mean nothing to you?

[VLADIMIR *and* ESTRAGON *look at each other questioningly.*]

ESTRAGON[*pretending to search*]: Bozzo . . . Bozz . . .

VLADIMIR[*ditto*]: Pozzo . . . Pozzo . . .

POZZO: PPPOZZZO!

ESTRAGON: Ah! Pozzo . . . let me see. Pozzo . . .

VLADIMIR: It is Pozzo or Bozzo?

ESTRAGON: Pozzo . . . no . . . I'm afraid I . . . no . . . I don't seem to . . .

[POZZO *advances threateningly.*]

VLADIMIR [*conciliating*]: I once knew a family called Gozzo. The mother had warts —

ESTRAGON: We're not from these parts, sir.

POZZO[*halting*]: You are human beings none the less. [*He puts on his spectacles.*] As far as one can see. [*He takes off his spectacles.*] Of the same species as myself. [*He bursts into an enormous laugh.*] Of the same species as Pozzo! Made in God's image!

VLADIMIR: Well you see —

POZZO[*peremptory*]: Who is Godot?

ESTRAGON: Godot?

POZZO: You took me for Godot.

ESTRAGON: Oh no, sir, not for an instant, sir.

POZZO: Who is he?

VLADIMIR: Oh, he's a . . . he's a kind of acquaintance.

ESTRAGON: Nothing of the kind, we hardly know him.

VLADIMIR: True . . . we don't know him very well . . . but all the same . . .

ESTRAGON: Personally, I wouldn't even know him if I saw him.

POZZO: You took me for him.

ESTRAGON [*recoiling before* POZZO]: That's to say . . . you understand . . . the dusk . . . the strain . . . waiting . . . I confess . . . I imagined . . . for a second . . .

POZZO: Waiting? So you were waiting for him?

VLADIMIR: Well you see —

POZZO: Here? on my land?

VLADIMIR: We didn't intend any harm.

ESTRAGON: We meant well.

POZZO: The road is free to all.

VLADIMIR: That's how we looked at it.

POZZO: It's a disgrace. But there you are.

ESTRAGON: Nothing we can do about it.

POZZO [*with magnanimous gesture*]: Let's say no more about it. [*He jerks the rope.*] Up pig! [*Pause.*] Every time he drops he falls asleep. [*Jerks the rope.*] Up hog! [*Noise of* LUCKY *getting up and picking up his baggage.* POZZO *jerks the rope.*] Back! [*Enter* LUCKY *backwards.*] Stop! [LUCKY *stops.*] Turn! [LUCKY *turns. To* VLADIMIR *and* ESTRAGON, *affably.*] Gentlemen, I am happy to have met you. [*Before their incredulous expression.*] Yes, yes, sincerely happy. [*He jerks the rope.*] Closer! [LUCKY *advances.*] Stop! [LUCKY *stops. To* VLADIMIR *and* ESTRAGON.] Yes, the road seems long when one journeys all alone for ... [*he consults his watch*] ... yes ... [*he calculates*] ... yes ... six hours, that's right, six hours on end, and never a soul in sight. [*To* LUCKY.] Coat! [LUCKY *puts down the bag, advances, gives the coat, goes back to his place, takes up the bag.*] Hold that! [POZZO *holds out the whip.* LUCKY *advances and, both his hands being occupied, takes the whip in his mouth, then goes back to his place.* POZZO *begins to put on his coat, stops.*] Coat! [LUCKY *puts down bag, basket and stool, advances, helps* POZZO *on with his coat, goes back to his place and takes up bag, basket and stool.*] Touch of autumn in the air this evening.

[POZZO *finishes buttoning his coat, stoops, inspects himself, straightens up.*] Whip! [LUCKY *advances, stoops,* POZZO *snatches the whip from his mouth,* LUCKY *goes back to his stool.*] Yes, gentlemen, I cannot go for long without the society of my likes. [*He puts on his glasses and looks at the two likes.*] Even when the likeness is an imperfect one. [*He takes off his glasses.*] Stool! [LUCKY *puts down bag and basket, advances, opens stool, puts it down, goes back to his place, takes up bag and basket.*] Closer! [POZZO *sits down, places the butt of his whip against* LUCKY's *chest and pushes.*] Back! [LUCKY *takes a step back.*] Further! [LUCKY *takes another step back.*] Stop! [LUCKY *stops. To* VLADIMIR *and* ESTRAGON.] That is why, with your permission, I propose to dally with you a moment, before I venture any further. Basket! [LUCKY *advances, gives the basket, goes back to his place.*] The fresh air stimulates the jaded appetite. [*He opens the basket, takes out a piece of chicken, a piece of bread and a bottle of wine.*] Basket! [LUCKY *advances, gives the basket, goes back to his place.*] Further! [LUCKY *takes a step back.*] He stinks. Happy days! [*He drinks from the bottle, puts it down, begins to eat. Silence.* VLADIMIR *and* ESTRAGON, *cautiously at first, then more boldly, begin to circle about* LUCKY, *inspecting him up and down.* POZZO *eats his chicken voraciously, throwing away the bones after having sucked them.* LUCKY *sags slowly, until bag and basket touch the ground, then straightens up with a start and begins to sag again. Rhythm of one sleeping on his feet.*]

ESTRAGON: What ails him?

VLADIMIR: He looks tired.

ESTRAGON: Why doesn't he put down his bags?

VLADIMIR: How do I know? [*They close in on him.*] Careful!

ESTRAGON: Say something to him.

VLADIMIR: Look!

ESTRAGON: What?

VLADIMIR [*pointing*]: His neck.

ESTRAGON [*looking at his neck*]: I see nothing.

VLADIMIR: Here.

[ESTRAGON *goes over beside* VLADIMIR.]

ESTRAGON: Oh, I say!

VLADIMIR: A running sore.

ESTRAGON: It's the rope.

VLADIMIR: It's the rubbing.

ESTRAGON: It's inevitable.

VLADIMIR: It's the knot.

ESTRAGON: It's the chafing.

[*They resume their inspection, dwell on the face.*]

VLADIMIR: He's not bad looking.

ESTRAGON [*shrugging his shoulders, wry face*]: Would you say so?

VLADIMIR: A trifle effeminate.

ESTRAGON: Look at the slobber.

Samuel Beckett

VLADIMIR: It's inevitable.

ESTRAGON: Look at the slaver.

VLADIMIR: Perhaps he's a half-wit.

ESTRAGON: A cretin.

VLADIMIR [*looking closer*]: It looks like a goitre.

ESTRAGON [*ditto*]: It's not certain.

VLADIMIR: He's panting.

ESTRAGON: It's inevitable.

VLADIMIR: And his eyes!

ESTRAGON: What about them?

VLADIMIR: Goggling out of his head.

ESTRAGON: Looks at his last gasp to me.

VLADIMIR: It's not certain. [*Pause.*] Ask him a question.

ESTRAGON: Would that be a good thing?

VLADIMIR: What do we risk?

ESTRAGON [*timidly*]: Mister . . .

VLADIMIR: Louder.

ESTRAGON [*louder*]: Mister . . .

POZZO: Leave him in peace! . . .

QUESTIONS AND DISCUSSION POINTS

1. How does Beckett suggest the universal, allegorical meaning of the situation?

2. In what respects does the dialogue conform to, and in what respects does it differ from, ordinary every-day speech.

3. How distinctly are the characters of Vladimir and Estragon differentiated in this episode?

4. Does the element of absurdity make an essential contribution to the success of this episode?

5. What do you think is the purpose of dwelling on the details of Pozzo's treatment of Lucky, and such details as the running sore?

6. Beckett wrote in 1931 that man hides behind 'the haze of our smug will to live, of our pernicious and incurable optimism.' Is this view of human life evident in this extract?

EUGÈNE IONESCO

Rhinoceros

Rhinoceros (1960) is one of the boldest imaginative strokes of th
modern anti-realistic Theatre of the Absurd. The play requires th
audience to 'suspend its disbelief,' to indulge its fantasies by imagin
ing a world increasingly inhabited by rhinoceroses. Yet the play is a
acute criticism of the inherent dangers of a mass civilization. Th
various shortcomings of contemporary society are each represente
by one of the characters who succumb to the lure of the spiritua
state symbolized by the rhinoceros.

Briefly, the play centres on the consciousness of the shabby
Chaplinesque hero, Berenger, a man disapproved of by his ambitiou
and socially respectable friends as dissolute, spineless and aimless
As the play opens, Berenger is being rebuked by his friend, Jean
for his failure to fulfil what Jean calls his social 'duty'. Berenger i
unimpressed by Jean's assertions of society's claims on him. On thi
scene impinges, hilariously, a herd of rhinoceros, an event which
understandably, causes indignant astonishment among the peopl
on stage. With the help of another character, the Logician, Jea
succeeds in rationalizing this phenomenon; Berenger remain
hazily apathetic. The Logician, as we shall learn later, represent
what Ionesco sees as one of the great dangers of modern society
its pseudo-intellectual approach to problems which require
personal, emotional approach. For each of the characters who op
for the rhinoceros state has a rational pretext for doing so. Only th
initially feckless, and subsequently incoherently emotional Berenge

is saved from the fate which overtakes the others. 'Life is a struggle, it's cowardly not to put up a fight!' shouts Jean to Berenger, worthy enough sentiments, but dangerous by being platitudinous. Ionesco seems to feel that if an axiom or principle is not to become dangerous, it must be, to use Keats's phase, 'proved on the pulse,' its truth *personally* realized. In *Rhinoceros* Ionesco presents a world in which clichés have taken the place of human emotions.

The second act begins with a scene of bureaucratic bickering among Mr Papillon, the head of this particular office, Mr Dudard, his assistant, and Botard, a former schoolmaster. This is a typical part of the world of enervating routine such as saps the individual's mental resources and prepares the way for the ascendancy of the rhinoceros. A sterile and pedantic discussion on the exact nature of a cat killed by a rhinoceros is interrupted by a distraught Mrs Boeuf, who informs those present that her husband, a member of the office, has left her, and that she has just been chased by a rhinoceros. She soon discovers that the rhinoceros is, in fact, her husband, and, drawn by wifely love — a seemingly worthy motive — she joins her husband, to become a rhinoceros, to the general disapproval of the office staff.

This scene sets the pattern; Jean, Papillon, the Logician, Botard, Dudard, all succumb, for ostensibly sound reasons, to the lure of the rhinoceros state. Jean, for example, is attracted by the value of 'Nature' despite Berenger's plea for 'the human individual, humanism,' words whose banality embarrasses Berenger though he is in no doubt as to the validity of the principle they denote. Discussing Botard's defection with Berenger, Dudard recalls Botard's last sententious words: 'What he said was: we must move with the times! Those were his last human words.' The tyrannical power of the cliché is once again illustrated. Last to forsake his humanity is Dudard. He too rationalizes his decision, declaring that he joins the rhinoceros only so as to understand how their minds work: 'I shall keep my mind clear.'

Dudard's departure leaves Berenger and his girl-friend, Daisy, together preparing the way for the final and most moving clash between clichés and sentimentality on the one hand and stubborn individuality on the other. Inevitably, clichés and sentimentality triumph, and Berenger is left alone in a world of rhinoceros, holding on grimly to an unshared humanity and expressing his tortured vacillations in a very moving final soliloquy.

The play, then, is a devastatingly funny criticism of the clichéridden, pseudo-intellectual conformism of modern society, a criticism made more effective by its brilliant use of one of the fundamental insights of Twentieth Century literature, the realization of the absurdity as well as the pathos of the human condition.

*   *   *   *   *

The extract which follows is the conclusion of the play, the final attempt by Berenger to hold on to Daisy, and his struggle with himself which culminates in his final determination to resist the temptations of the rhinoceros state.

Extract from *Rhinoceros*

Pp. 117–124 of Penguin edition.

(First published by John Calder).

BERENGER [*he, too, is afraid*]: Don't be frightened, my dear. We're together — you're happy with me, aren't you? It's enough that I'm with you isn't it? I'll chase all your fears away.

DAISY: Perhaps it's all our own fault.

BERENGER: Don't think about it any longer. We mustn't start feeling remorse. It's dangerous to start feeling guilty. We must just live our lives, and be happy. We have the right to be happy. They're not spiteful, and we're not doing them any harm. They'll leave us in peace. You just keep calm and rest. Sit in the armchair. [*He leads her to the armchair.*] Just keep calm! [*Daisy sits in the armchair.*] Would you like a drop of brandy to pull you together?

DAISY: I've got a headache.

BERENGER [*taking up his bandage and binding DAISY's head*]: I love you, my darling. Don't you worry, they'll get over it. It's just a passing phase.

DAISY: They won't get over it. It's for good.

BERENGER: I love you. I love you madly.

DAISY [*taking off the bandage*]: Let things just take their course. What can we do about it?

BERENGER: They've all gone mad. The world is sick. They're all sick.

DAISY: We shan't be the ones to cure them.

BERENGER: How can we live in the same house with them?

DAISY [*calming down*]: We must be sensible. We must adapt ourselves and try and get on with them.

BERENGER: They can't understand us.

DAISY: They must. There's no other way.

BERENGER: Do you understand them?

DAISY: Not yet. But we must try to understand the way their minds work, and learn their language.

127

BERENGER: They haven't got a language! Listen ... do you call that a language?

DAISY: How do you know? You're no polyglot!

BERENGER: We'll talk about it later. We must have lunch first.

DAISY: I'm not hungry any more. It's all too much. I can't take any more.

BERENGER: But you're the strong one. You're not going to let it get you down. It's precisely for your courage that I admire you so.

DAISY: You said that before.

BERENGER: Do you feel sure of my love?

DAISY: Yes, of course.

BERENGER: I love you so.

DAISY: You keep saying the same thing, my dear.

BERENGER: Listen, Daisy, there *is* something we can do. We'll have children, and our children will have children — it'll take time, but together we can regenerate the human race.

DAISY: Regenerate the human race?

BERENGER: It happened once before.

DAISY: Ages ago. Adam and Eve ... They had a lot of courage.

BERENGER: And we, too, can have courage. We don't need all that much. It happens automatically with time and patience.

DAISY: What's the use?

BERENGER: Of course we can — with a little bit of courage.

DAISY: I don't want to have children — it's a bore.

BERENGER: How can we save the world, if you don't?

DAISY: Why bother to save it?

BERENGER: What a thing to say! Do it for me, Daisy. Let's save the world.

DAISY: After all, perhaps it's we who need saving. Perhaps we're the abnormal ones.

BERENGER: You're not yourself, Daisy, you've got a touch of fever.

DAISY: There aren't any more of our kind about anywhere, are there?

BERENGER: Daisy, you're not to talk like that!

[DAISY *looks all around at the rhinoceros heads on the walls, on the landing door, and now starting to appear along the footlights.*]

DAISY: Those are the real people. They look happy. They're content to be what they are. They don't look insane. They look very natural. They were right to do what they did.

BERENGER [*clasping his hands and looking despairingly at* DAISY]: We're the ones who are doing right, Daisy, I assure you.

DAISY: That's very presumptuous of you!

BERENGER: You know perfectly well I'm right.

DAISY: There's no such thing as absolute right. It's the world that's right — not you and me.

BERENGER: I *am* right, Daisy. And the proof is that you understand me when I speak to you.

DAISY: What does that prove?

BERENGER: The proof is that I love you as much as it's possible for a man to love a woman.

DAISY: Funny sort of argument.

BERENGER: I don't understand you any longer, Daisy. You don't know what you're saying, darling. Think of our love! Our love . . .

DAISY: I feel a bit ashamed of what you call love — this morbid feeling, this male weakness. And female, too. It just doesn't compare with the ardour and the tremendous energy emanating from all these creatures around us.

BERENGER: Energy! You want some energy, do you? I can let you have some energy! [*He slaps her face.*]

DAISY: Oh! I never would have believed it possible . . . [*She sinks into the armchair.*]

BERENGER: Oh forgive me, my darling, please forgive me! [*He tries to embrace her, she evades him.*] Forgive me, my darling. I didn't mean it. I don't know what came over me, losing control like that!

DAISY: It's because you've run out of arguments, that's why.

BERENGER: Oh dear! In the space of a few minutes we've gone through twenty-five years of married life.

DAISY: I pity you. I understand you all too well . . .

BERENGER [*as* DAISY *weeps*]: You're probably right that I've run out of arguments. You think they're stronger than me, stronger than us. Maybe they are.

DAISY: Indeed they are.

BERENGER: Well, in spite of everything, I swear to you I'll never give in, never!

DAISY [*she rises, goes to* BERENGER, *puts her arms round his neck*]: My poor darling, I'll help you to resist — to the very end.

BERENGER: Will you be capable of it?

DAISY: I give you my word. You can trust me [*The rhinoceros noises have become melodious.*] Listen, they're singing!

BERENGER: They're not singing, they're roaring.

DAISY: They're singing.

BERENGER: They're roaring, I tell you.

DAISY: You're mad, they're singing.

BERENGER: You can't have a very musical ear, then.

DAISY: You don't know the first thing about music, poor dear — and look, they're playing as well, and dancing.

BERENGER: You call that dancing?

DAISY: It's their way of dancing. They're beautiful.

BERENGER: They're disgusting!

DAISY: You're not to say unpleasant things about them. It upsets me.

BERENGER: I'm sorry. We're not going to quarrel on their account.

DAISY: They're like gods.

BERENGER: You go too far, Daisy; take a good look at them.

DAISY: You mustn't be jealous, my dear.

[*She goes to* BERENGER *again and tries to embrace him. This time it is* BERENGER *who frees himself.*]

BERENGER: I can see our opinions are directly opposed. It's better not to discuss the matter.

DAISY: Now you mustn't be nasty.

BERENGER: Then don't you be stupid!

DAISY [*to* BERENGER, *who turns his back on her. He looks at himself closely in the mirror*]: It's no longer possible for us to live together. [*As* BERENGER *continues to examine himself in the mirror she goes quietly to the door, saying*] He isn't very nice really, he isn't very nice. [*She goes out, and is seen slowly descending the stairs.*]

BERENGER [*still looking at himself in the mirror*]: Men aren't so bad-looking, you know. And I'm not a particularly handsome specimen! Believe me, Daisy! [*He turns round.*] Daisy! Daisy! Where are you, Daisy? You can't do that to me! [*He darts to the door.*] Daisy! [*He gets to the landing and leans over the banister.*] Daisy! Come back! Come back, my dear! You haven't even had your lunch, Daisy, don't leave me alone! Remember your promise! Daisy! Daisy! [*He stops calling, makes a despairing gesture, and comes back into the room.*] Well it was obvious we weren't getting along together. The home was broken up. It just wasn't working out. But she shouldn't have left like that with no explanation.[*He looks all round.*] She didn't even leave a message. That's no way to behave. Now I'm all on my own. [*He locks the door carefully, but angrily.*] But they won't get me! [*He carefully closes the windows.*] You won't get me. [*He addresses all the rhinoceros heads.*] I'm not joining you; I don't understand you! I'm staying as I am. I'm a human being. A human being. [*He sits in the armchair.*] It's an impossible situation. It's my fault she's gone. I meant everything to her. What'll become of her? That's one more person on my conscience. I can easily picture the worst, because the worst can easily happen. Poor little thing left all alone in this world of monsters! Nobody can help me find her, nobody, because there's nobody left.

[*Fresh trumpetings, hectic racings, clouds of dust.*]

I can't bear the sound of them any longer, I'm going to put cotton wool in my ears. [*He does so, and talks to himself in the mirror.*] The only solution is to convince them — but convince them of what? Are the changes reversible, that's the point? Are they reversible? It would be a labour of Hercules, far beyond me. In any case, to convince them you'd have to talk to them. And to talk to them I'd have to learn their language. Or they'd have to learn mine. But what language do I speak? What is my language? Am I talking French? Yes, it must be French. But what is French? I can call it French if I want, and nobody can say it isn't — I'm the only one who speaks it. What am I saying? Do I understand what I'm saying? Do I? [*He crosses to the middle of the room.*] And what if it's true what Daisy said, and they're the ones in the right? [*He turns back to the mirror.*] A man's not ugly to look at,

not ugly at all. [*He examines himself, passing his hand over his face.*]
What a funny-looking thing! What do I look like? What?
[*He darts to a cupboard, takes out some photographs which he examines.*] Photographs? Who are all these people? Is it Mr Papillon
— or is it Daisy? And is that Botard or Dudard or Jean? Or is it
me? [*He rushes to the cupboard again and takes out two or three
pictures.*] Now I recognize me: that's me, that's me. [*He hangs the
pictures on the back wall, beside the rhinoceros heads.*] That's me,
that's me!

[*When he hangs the pictures one sees that they are of an old man, a huge
woman, and another man. The ugliness of these pictures is in contrast
to the rhinoceros heads which have become very beautiful.* BERENGER
steps back to contemplate the pictures.]

I'm not good-looking, I'm not good-looking. [*He takes down the
pictures, throws them furiously to the ground, and goes over to the
mirror.*] They're the good-looking ones. I was wrong! Oh, how I
wish I was like them! I haven't got any horns, more's the pity!
A smooth brow looks so ugly. I need one or two horns to give
my sagging face a lift. Perhaps one will grow and I needn't be
ashamed any more — then I could go and join them. But it will
never grow! [*He looks at the palms of his hands.*] My hands are so
limp — oh, why won't they get rough! [*He takes his coat off,
undoes his shirt to look at his chest in the mirror.*] My skin is so slack.
I can't stand this white, hairy body. Oh, I'd love to have a hard
skin in that wonderful dull green colour — a skin that looks
decent naked without any hair on it, like theirs! [*He listens to their
trumpetings.*] Their song is charming — a bit raucous perhaps, but
it does have charm! I wish I could do it! [*He tries to imitate them.*]
Ahh, Ahh, Brr! No, that's not it! Try again, louder! Ahh, Ahh,
Brr! No, that's not it, it's too feeble, it's got no drive behind it.
I'm not trumpeting at all; I'm just howling. Ahh, Ahh, Brr.
There's a big difference between howling and trumpeting. I've
only myself to blame; I should have gone with them while there
was still time. Now it's too late! Now I'm a monster, just a
monster. Now I'll never become a rhinoceros, never, never!
I'm gone past changing. I want to, I really do, but I can't, I just

can't. I can't stand the sight of me. I'm too ashamed! [*He turns his back on the mirror.*] I'm so ugly! People who try to hang on to their individuality always come to a bad end! [*He suddenly snaps out of it.*] Oh well, too bad! I'll take on the whole of them! I'll put up a fight against the lot of them, the whole lot of them! I'm the last man left, and I'm staying that way until the end. I'm not capitulating!

CURTAIN

QUESTIONS AND DISCUSSION POINTS

1. On the evidence of this extract, can Berenger legitimately be said to possess genuinely heroic qualities?

2. What are the main temptations which Berenger has to resist in his struggle against 'capitulation'? What aspects of these temptations does Daisy represent?

3. Do you think that the length and complexity of Berenger's final soliloquy is dramatically justifiable?

4. Point out the elements of 'absurdity' which Ionesco uses in this passage.

5. Do you feel that there is any conflict between the serious point which Ionesco is attempting to convey and the comedy of the absurd through which it is conveyed?

6. What main aspect of Twentieth Century life is Ionesco concerned with here? Does he make the state symbolized by the rhinoceros seem really threatening?

HAROLD PINTER

The Caretaker

As its title implies, in a characteristic pun, *The Caretaker* (1959), is a play about a group of men who take great care not to reveal anything about their deepest hopes and needs. The central character is particularly ingenious and pathetic in his efforts to hide from others the facts of his life. This, then, is not a play about 'failure of communication,' but rather about man's desire to confine speech to the enunciation of commonplaces so that he can remain cocooned within himself.

The play offers us very little in the way of traditional characterization or plot. It is about the relationships which flicker sporadically among three people, a tramp, Davies, and two brothers, Aston and Mick. Aston offers Davies a bed in his room and tries to strike up some kind of friendship with him. Davies, however, is suspicious and fends off all enquiries with lies about the prospects which await him if he can get to Sidcup and claim his means of identity, his 'papers'. Typical of his suspicion is the fact that for a large part of the play he assumes the name of Jenkins. While staying in the room, Davies is terrorized by the unbalanced and sadistic Mick who alternately confides in him about his brother and the mysterious 'treatment' he has had, and rejects and jeers at him. Finally, Mick, who owns the house tells Davies that he will have to go; Davies is driven almost to the point of pleading with Mick to let him stay but finally in the face of the adamant refusal of both brothers to show any mercy he has to leave the Paradise which he has almost gained. He is rejected, as he had been accepted, for no rational or specific point. As he wanders away we begin to realize the implications of what we have witnessed, the human failure of relationship in which we are all involved.

Before he turned to writing plays in the mid-fifties, Pinter was himself an actor, and this play shows an immense grasp of the dramatic possibilities of the simplest situation. Darkness and light, speech and silence, space and the lack of it, all are superbly used. The two brothers, for example, address each other only when they must, and then very briefly. There is a wonderfully terrifying scene which is enacted in darkness and almost in silence as Mick uses an Electrolux sweeper in a dark room to terrify Davies. On the other hand, there is Aston's terrifying and stumbling recollections of the treatment to which he was subjected in a mental hospital, with which Act Two ends. And this is perhaps Pinter's greatest achievement; he has achieved a style which is capable of the subtlest modulations, in which the prosaic is always merging into the terrifying. No other living dramatist conveys such a sense of the constant possibility of the irruption of the unknown and the destructive into our daily lives.

*   *   *   *   *

The following episode occurs just after Davies has been, hilariously and terrifyingly, chased around a darkened room by Mick, armed with an Electrolux. Characteristically, after treating him sadistically, Mick lures Davies into a false sense of security.

Extract from *The Caretaker*

Pp. 46–52 of Methuen edition.

DAVIES: You come near me . . . .

MICK: I'm sorry if I gave you a start. But I had you in mind too, you know. I mean, my brother's guest. We got to think of your comfort, en't we? Don't want the dust to get up your nose. How long you thinking of staying here, by the way? As a matter of fact, I was going to suggest that we'd lower your rent, make it just a nominal sum, I mean until you get fixed up. Just nominal, that's all.

[*Pause.*]

Still, if you're going to be spiky, I'll have to reconsider the whole proposition.

[*Pause.*]

Eh, you're not thinking of doing any violence on me, are you? You're not the violent sort, are you?

DAVIES [*vehemently*]: I keep myself to myself, mate. But if anyone starts with me though, they know what they got coming.

MICK: I can believe that.

DAVIES: You do. I been all over, see? You understand my meaning? I don't mind a bit of a joke now and then, but anyone'll tell you . . . that no one starts anything with me.

MICK: I get what you mean, yes.

DAVIES: I can be pushed so far . . . but . . .

MICK: No further.

DAVIES: That's it.

[MICK *sits on junk down right.*]

What you doing?

MICK: No, I just want to say that . . . I'm very impressed by that.

DAVIES: Eh?

MICK: I'm very impressed by what you've just said.

[*Pause.*] Yes, that's impressive, that is.

[*Pause.*] I'm impressed, anyway.

136

DAVIES: You know what I'm talking about, then?

MICK: Yes, I know. I think we understand one another.

DAVIES: Uh? Well . . . I'll tell you . . . I'd . . . I'd like to think that. You been playing me about, you know. I don't know why. I never done you no harm.

MICK: No, you know what it was? We just got off on the wrong foot. That's all it was.

DAVIES: Ay, we did.

[DAVIES *joins* MICK *in junk.*]

MICK: Like a sandwich?

DAVIES: What?

MICK [*taking a sandwich from his pocket*]: Have one of these.

DAVIES: Don't you pull anything.

MICK: No, you're still not understanding me. I can't help being interested in any friend of my brother's. I mean, you're my brother's friend, aren't you?

DAVIES: Well, I . . . I wouldn't put it as far as that.

MICK: Don't you find him friendly, then?

DAVIES: Well, I wouldn't say we was all that friends. I mean, he done me no harm, but I wouldn't say he was any particular friend of mine. What's in that sandwich, then?

MICK: Cheese.

DAVIES: That'll do me.

MICK: Take one.

DAVIES: Thank you, mister.

MICK: I'm sorry to hear my brother's not very friendly.

DAVIES: He's friendly, he's friendly, I didn't say he wasn't . . .

MICK [*taking a salt-cellar from his pocket*]: Salt?

DAVIES: No thanks. [*He munches the sandwich.*] I just can't exactly . . . make him out.

MICK [*feeling in his pocket*]: I forgot the pepper.

DAVIES: Just can't get the hang of him, that's all.

MICK: I had a bit of beetroot somewhere. Must have mislaid it. [*Pause.*]

[DAVIES *chews the sandwich.* MICK *watches him eat. He then rises and strolls downstage.*]

Uuh ... listen ... can I ask your advice? I mean, you're a man
of the world. Can I ask your advice about something?

DAVIES: You go right ahead.

MICK: Well, what it is, you see, I'm ... I'm a bit worried about my
brother.

DAVIES: Your brother?

MICK: Yes ... you see, his trouble is ...

DAVIES: What?

MICK: Well, it's not a very nice thing to say ...

DAVIES [*rising, coming downstage*]: Go on now, you say it.

[MICK *looks at him.*]

MICK: He doesn't like work.

[*Pause.*]

DAVIES: Go on!

MICK: No, he just doesn't like work, that's his trouble.

DAVIES: Is that a fact?

MICK: It's a terrible thing to have to say about your own brother.

DAVIES: Ay.

MICK: He's just shy of it. Very shy of it.

DAVIES: I know that sort.

MICK: You know the type?

DAVIES: I've met them.

MICK: I mean, I want to get him going in the world.

DAVIES: Stands to reason, man.

MICK: If you got an older brother you want to push him on, you
want to see him make his way. Can't have him idle, he's only
doing himself harm. That's what I say.

DAVIES: Yes.

MICK: But he won't buckle down to the job.

DAVIES: He don't like work.

MICK: Work shy.

DAVIES: Sounds like it to me.

MICK: You've met the type, have you?

DAVIES: Me? I know that sort.

MICK: Yes.

DAVIES: I know that sort. I've met them.

MICK: Causing me great anxiety. You see, I'm a working man: I'm a tradesman. I've got my own van.

DAVIES: Is that a fact?

MICK: He's supposed to be doing a little job for me . . . I keep him here to do a little job . . . but I don't know . . . I'm coming to the conclusion he's a slow worker.

[*Pause.*] What would your advice be?

DAVIES: Well . . . he's a funny bloke, your brother.

MICK: What?

DAVIES: I was saying, he's . . . he's a bit of a funny bloke; your brother.

[MICK *stares at him.*]

MICK: Funny? Why?

DAVIES: Well . . . he's funny . . .

MICK: What's funny about him?

[*Pause.*]

DAVIES: Not liking work.

MICK: What's funny about that?

DAVIES: Nothing.

[*Pause.*]

MICK: I don't call it funny.

DAVIES: Nor me.

MICK: You don't want to start getting hypercritical.

DAVIES: No, no, I wasn't that, I wasn't . . . I was only saying . . .

MICK: Don't get too glib.

DAVIES: Look, all I meant was —

MICK: Cut it! [*Briskly.*] Look! I got a proposition to make to you. I'm thinking of taking over the running of this place, you see? I think it could be run a bit more efficiently. I got a lot of ideas, a lot of plans. [*He eyes* DAVIES.] How would you like to stay on here, as caretaker?

DAVIES: What?

MICK: I'll be quite open with you. I could rely on a man like you around the place, keeping an eye on things.

DAVIES: Well now . . . wait a minute . . . I . . . I ain't never done no caretaking before, you know . . .

MICK: Doesn't matter about that. It's just that you look a capable sort of man to me.

DAVIES: I am a capable sort of man. I mean to say, I've had plenty offers in my time, you know, there's no getting away from that.

MICK: Well, I could see before, when you took out that knife, that you wouldn't let anyone mess you about.

DAVIES: No one messes me about, man.

MICK: I mean, you've been in the services, haven't you?

DAVIES: The what?

MICK: You been in the services. You can tell by your stance.

DAVIES: Oh . . . yes. Spent half my life there, man. Overseas . . . like . . . serving . . . I was.

MICK: In the colonies, weren't you?

DAVIES: I was over there. I was one of the first over there.

MICK: That's it. You're just the man I been looking for.

DAVIES: What for?

MICK: Caretaker.

DAVIES: Yes, well . . . look . . . listen . . . who's the landlord here, him or you?

MICK: Me. I am. I got deeds to prove it.

DAVIES: Ah . . . [*Decisively.*] Well listen, I don't mind doing a bit of caretaking, I wouldn't mind looking after the place for you.

MICK: Of course, we'd come to a small financial agreement, mutually beneficial.

DAVIES: I leave you to reckon that out, like.

MICK: Thanks. There's only one thing.

DAVIES: What's that?

MICK: Can you give me any references?

DAVIES: Eh?

MICK: Just to satisfy my solicitor.

DAVIES: I got plenty of references. All I got to do is to go down to Sidcup tomorrow. I got all the references I want down there.

MICK: Where's that?

DAVIES: Sidcup. He ain't only got my references down there, he got all my papers down there. I know that place like the back of my hand. I'm going down there anyway, see what I mean, I got to get down there, or I'm done.

MICK: So we can always get hold of these references if we want them.

DAVIES: I'll be down there any day, I tell you. I was going down today, but I'm . . . I'm waiting for the weather to break.

MICK: Ah.

DAVIES: Listen. You can't pick me up a pair of good shoes, can you? I got a bad need for a good pair of shoes. I can't get anywhere without a pair of good shoes, see? Do you think there's any chance of you being able to pick me up a pair?

THE LIGHTS FADE TO BLACKOUT

QUESTIONS AND DISCUSSION POINTS

1. 'The more acute the experience, the less articulate its expression'; 'Communication itself between people is so frightening that rather than do that there is a continual cross-talk, a continual talking about other things, rather than what is at the root of their relationship.' Do these statements of Pinter's seem to you true in themselves? Consider their relevance to *The Caretaker*.

2. What prevents the dialogue from becoming trivial and boring?

3. What is our attitude towards the two characters? How does Pinter control this attitude?

4. How does Pinter suggest menace, fear and mistrust?

5. Are there any moments which are simply funny?

6. Try to define how Pinter excites our interest in characters who reveal so little of themselves.

SUGGESTIONS FOR FURTHER READING

1. Further reading of the dramatists included in this book might begin with the following plays, most of which are available in paperbacked editions:

IBSEN, *The Wild Duck*
STRINDBERG, *The Father*
CHEKHOV, *The Cherry Orchard*
SHAW, *Major Barbara*
SYNGE, *Deirdre of the Sorrows*
O'CASEY, *The Plough and the Stars*
BRECHT, *The Caucasian Chalk Circle*
MILLER, *The Crucible*
WESKER, *Chips with Everything*
BECKETT, *Happy Days*
IONESCO, *Chairs*
PINTER, *The Birthday Party*.

2. Among critical works on modern drama the following are stimulating:

ROBERT BRUSTEIN, *The Theatre of Revolt*
JOSEPH CHIARI, *Landmarks of Contemporary Drama*
NIGEL DENNIS, *Dramatic Essays*
MARTIN ESSLIN, *The Theatre of the Absurd*
BAMBER GASCOIGNE, *Twentieth Century Drama*
KENNETH TYNAN, *Curtains*
RAYMOND WILLIAMS, *Drama from Ibsen to Eliot*.

3. A very useful collection of modern dramatists' statements of their aims is:

TOBY COLE, *Playwrights on Playwriting*.

4. The following plays will help to show the range of recent drama:

JOHN ARDEN, *Sergeant Musgrave's Dance*
ROBERT BOLT, *A Man for All Seasons*
FRIEDRICH DÜRRENMATT, *The Physicists*
MAX FRISCH, *The Fireraisers*
HENRY LIVINGS, *Eh?*
JOHN OSBORNE, *The Entertainer*
N. F. SIMPSON, *A Resounding Tinkle*.